THE EIGHT
DOORS
of the
Kingdom

D1519411

THE EIGHT
DOORS
of the
Kingdom

MEDITATION ON
THE BEATITUDES

JACQUES PHILIPPE

 Scepter

Blessed are the poor in spirit, for theirs is the kingdom of heaven.

Blessed are those who mourn, for they shall be comforted.

Blessed are the meek, for they shall inherit the earth.

Blessed are those who hunger and thirst for righteousness, for they shall be satisfied.

Blessed are the merciful, for they shall obtain mercy.

Blessed are the pure in heart, for they shall see God.

Blessed are the peacemakers, for they shall be called sons of God.

Blessed are those who are persecuted for righteousness' sake, for theirs is the kingdom of heaven.

Blessed are you when men revile you and persecute you and utter all kinds of evil against you falsely on my account.

Rejoice and be glad, for your reward is great in heaven, for so men persecuted the prophets who were before you.

Originally published as *Le bonheur où on ne l'attend pas: Méditation sur les Béatitudes*. Copyright © 2017 Éditions des Béatitudes, S.O.C., Burtin, France.

This English version *The Eight Doors of the Kingdom: Meditations on the Beatitudes* is copyright © 2018 Scepter Publishers, Inc.

Published by Scepter Publishers, Inc.
info@scepterpublishers.org
www.scepterpublishers.org
800-322-8773
New York

Text and cover design by Rose Design

Library of Congress Cataloging-in-Publication Data

 Names: Philippe, Jacques, 1947- author.
Title: The eight doors of the kingdom : meditations on the Beatitudes /
 Jacques Philippe.
Other titles: Bonheur où on ne l'attend pas. English
Description: New York : Scepter Publishers, 2018. | Description based on
 print version record and CIP data provided by publisher; resource not
 viewed.
Identifiers: LCCN 2018003825 (print) | LCCN 2018004604 (ebook) | ISBN
 9781594172762 (ebook) | ISBN 9781594172755 (pbk.)
Subjects: LCSH: Beatitudes--Meditations.
Classification: LCC BT382 (ebook) | LCC BT382 .P4813 2018 (print) | DDC
 226.9/306--dc23
LC record available at https://lccn.loc.gov/2018003825

Printed in the United States of America

PB ISBN: 9781594172755   eBook ISBN: 9781594172762

CONTENTS

INTRODUCTION

In this book, without theological pretensions or any particular exegesis, I propose a meditation on the Beatitudes found in Matthew's Gospel,[1] especially the first, poorness of spirit: *Blessed are the poor in spirit, for theirs is the kingdom of heaven.* A lot has been written on this topic, but it is so important for the life of the Church that we need always to return to it. Pope Francis ceaselessly exhorts Christians to live the Beatitudes, the only way of true happiness and also the only way to rebuild society.

Today's world is sick with pride, with insatiable desire for riches and domination, and cannot be healed except by accepting this message. To be faithful to the mission Christ entrusted to the Church, to be "*salt of the earth*" and "*light of the world,*"[2] the Church must be poor, humble, meek, and merciful.

---

1. Mt 5:1–12.
2. Mt 5:13–14.

We are strongly called to hear this essential teaching of Jesus, which we may not have truly understood or put into practice. As the Church continues its pilgrimage through history, it is increasingly summoned to radiate the spirit of the Beatitudes, giving off "*the aroma of Christ.*"[3] The Holy Spirit means to act forcefully to this end, even if doing so sometimes stirs up the Church. Every Christian must give off the perfume of the Gospel, an aroma of peace and meekness, of joy and humility.

More and more I am convinced that poorness of spirit is the key to the spiritual life, indeed to any path toward saintliness and fruitfulness. The Beatitudes contain liberating and enlightening wisdom, yet they are among those parts of the Gospel that we have the most difficulty understanding and putting into practice. Even among Christians one finds a tendency to think too much in terms of riches, quantity, or measurable efficiencies. The Gospel invites us to adopt a very different attitude.

---

3. 2 Cor 2:15.

A Holistic View of this Gospel

Before looking one by one at each of the Beatitudes, I want to say something about them as a whole.

This Gospel passage isn't easy to understand. It is paradoxical, even shocking. When I was a young priest, it was difficult for me to preach on the Beatitudes. But little by little I came to realize that this is an extraordinary text, one that encompasses all the novelty of the Gospel, all its wisdom and its power to transform profoundly the hearts of men and renew the world.

We must, of course, read Jesus' words in their context. The Beatitudes come after verses in Matthew's gospel describing the crowds flocking to listen to Jesus:

> And he went about all Galilee, teaching in their synagogues and preaching the gospel of the kingdom and healing every disease and every infirmity among the people. So his fame spread throughout all Syria, and they brought him all the sick, those afflicted with various diseases and pains, demoniacs, epileptics, and paralytics, and he healed them. And great crowds followed him from Galilee and the Decap´olis and Jerusalem and Judea and from beyond the Jordan.[4]

---

4. Mt 4:23–25.

Seeing the crowds, Jesus climbs the mountain, sits down, lets his disciples approach him, and begins to teach by proclaiming the Beatitudes.

The crowds that gather around Jesus are thirsty for healing, for light, for happiness. He responds to this thirst; he gives these suffering people a magnificent promise of happiness, repeated nine times but in language very different from what we might expect. What he proposes isn't a human happiness, the image of happiness we are accustomed to, but an unexpected happiness, encountered in situations and attitudes not normally associated with happiness—a happiness that is not a human production but a "surprise from God," granted precisely when and where we thought it impossible.

Notice that through the image of salt and light, Jesus' first words after the Beatitudes evoke the singular grace that rests on his disciples and to which they must be faithful:

> You are the salt of the earth; but if salt has lost its taste, how shall its saltness be restored? It is no longer good for anything except to be thrown out and trodden under foot by men. You are the light of the world. A city set on a hill cannot be hid. Nor do men

light a lamp and put it under a bushel, but on a stand, and it gives light to all in the house. Let your light so shine before men, that they may see your good works and give glory to your Father who is in heaven.[5]

Jesus is quite aware of his disciples' human limits and failings, which the Gospel stories do just the reverse of attempting to conceal. But he doesn't hesitate to affirm that, without the witness of their lives, human existence would not have any appeal or make sense, and the world would fall into deep darkness. Evidently it is precisely in living the Beatitudes that they can fulfill this vocation of service to the world. Only the Gospel of the Beatitudes gives human existence its full meaning and truth.

In Matthew's gospel the Beatitudes form the introduction to the Sermon on the Mount, which is covered in chapters 5 to 7. This, Jesus' first major discourse, presents him as the new Moses who proclaims the new covenant of the Kingdom. Not, however, from the heights of Mount Sinai, smoking and quaking, in *thunders and lightnings, and a thick cloud*[6] but, as tradition

---

5. Mt 5:13–16.

6. Ex 19:16.

says, on a little hill on the banks of the Sea of Galilee. Yet this doesn't prevent Jesus from speaking with force and authority, an authority that surprised the crowd in that it was so different from the way the rabbis of the day taught. Several times he says, "*You have heard that it was said . . . , but I say to you . . .*" Yet he insists that he has not come to "*abolish the law and the prophets . . . but to fulfil them.*"[7]

The Sermon on the Mount concludes with the parable of two houses, one built on rock and the other on sand. This is a vibrant exhortation not to be content with saying "Lord, Lord" to this New Covenant but to put it into practice, thus doing the will of the Father who is in heaven.[8]

This New Covenant Jesus promulgates on the mount of the Beatitudes is not just a moral law, even though it obviously has strong implications for the domain of human behavior. Even more deeply than a code of conduct, no matter how exalted, it is a path toward the happiness of the Kingdom, an itinerary for union with God and personal interior renewal. It proposes a way of identification with Christ, of discovery

---

7. Mt 5:17.
8. Mt 7:21, 24–27.

of the Father, of openness to the Holy Spirit. Only the Spirit can give us true understanding of the Beatitudes, and only the Spirit makes it possible for us to apply them in our lives.

THE TRINITY IN THE BEATITUDES

The Trinitarian mystery present in the Gospel of the Beatitudes deserves our particular attention. More than a guide for conduct, it is first of all a profound, unexpected, and surprising new revelation of the very mystery of God.

A first reading makes it clear that the eight Beatitudes in St. Matthew (eight if we consider the ninth a repetition and amplification of the eighth) are above all a portrait of Jesus himself. "*The Beatitudes are not only a map for Christian life, but are the secret to Jesus' heart itself.*"[9] One could spend a long time explaining and meditating on how Christ, in his entire life and particularly in his Passion, is really the one who is poor in spirit—the only one who has integrally lived each of the Beatitudes, which are fully realized on the Cross.

---

9. Jean-Claude Sagne, *La quête de Dieu, chemin de guérison* (Paris: Éditions de l'Emmanuel, 2005), p. 89.

On Calvary, Jesus was absolutely poor, afflicted, meek, hungry, and thirsty for justice, merciful, pure of heart, a maker of peace, persecuted for justice. Practicing each of the Beatitudes to perfection, he received in fullness, through his resurrection and glorification, the promised reward, the joy of the Kingdom of Heaven. Greater yet, he received power to admit into his Kingdom any man or woman, even the greatest of sinners, as we see him in his encounter with the good thief, when, only a few moments before his death, Jesus promises this man who has invoked him with faith: "*Truly, I say to you, today you will be with me in Paradise.*"[10]

Jesus affirms in John's Gospel: "*who has seen me has seen the Father.*"[11] Thus the Beatitudes also show us the true face of the Father. They are the revelation of a new face of God—a face that has nothing to do with human fabrications and projections. They reveal God's incredible humility and infinite mercy. Yes, the Father is infinitely rich and all powerful, but there is also a mystery of poverty in the divine being, since he is nothing but love and mercy, entirely giving of self in order to make others exist. Like the father in the parable of

---

10. Lk 23:43.
11. Jn 14:9.

the prodigal son in Luke's Gospel, he lives not for himself but for his children.

The Father occupies an important place in the Sermon on the Mount. Here is where Jesus teaches the Our Father and where he extends this gentle invitation: "*But when you pray, go into your room and shut the door and pray to your Father who is in secret; and your Father who sees in secret will reward you.*"[12] Here, too, is where he invites us to abandon ourselves with confidence to the Lord's providence, without worrying about tomorrow, because "*your heavenly Father knows that you need [all these things].*"[13] And toward the end of the sermon, as we've seen, Jesus asks us to put his words into practice, inasmuch as they express "*the will of my Father who is in heaven.*"[14]

It appears, then, that the Sermon on the Mount and particularly the Beatitudes are a gift of the Father's mercy, a promise of grace, of interior transformation, of a new heart. The New Covenant proclaimed by Jesus is much more demanding than the old one, for it asks of us not merely adherence to external norms but a

---

12. Mt 6:6.

13. Mt 6:32.

14. Mt 7:21.

truth, a purity, and a sincerity that touch the depths of the human heart. "*For I tell you, unless your righteousness exceeds that of the scribes and Pharisees, you will never enter the kingdom of heaven.*"[15] Jesus demands a profound interior conversion reaching to the most intimate and secret depths of the heart.

We understand nothing of this New Covenant established by Jesus if we miss the point that it is more demanding—an unheard-of demand in that it calls on us to imitate God himself ("*You, therefore, must be perfect, as your heavenly Father is perfect.*"),[16] while bestowing as a gift from the merciful Father an extraordinary promise of interior transformation by the grace of the Holy Spirit: the greater requirement is a sign of a greater promise. For God gives us what he commands. The justice surpassing the Old Covenant to which Jesus calls us in the New Covenant is possible in light of the revelation of the Father's love, the example of Jesus, the outpouring of the Holy Spirit.

The promise of the New Covenant, foretold by Jeremiah, is fulfilled in the teaching of the Gospel, in which the Holy Spirit will come to the aid of the weakness of

---

15. Mt 5:20.
16. Mt 5:48.

mankind, and write God's law on our hearts, so that we finally become capable of accomplishing it:

> "Behold, the days are coming, says the LORD, when I will make a new covenant with the house of Israel and the house of Judah, not like the covenant which I made with their fathers when I took them by the hand to bring them out of the land of Egypt, my covenant which they broke, though I was their husband, says the LORD. But this is the covenant which I will make with the house of Israel after those days, says the LORD: I will put my law within them, and I will write it upon their hearts; and I will be their God, and they shall be my people."[17]

Consider, too, these words of Ezekiel: *"A new heart I will give you, and a new spirit I will put within you; and I will take out of your flesh the heart of stone and give you a heart of flesh."*[18]

The Beatitudes are a description of this "new heart" that the Holy Spirit fashions in us, which is the very heart of Christ.

---

17. Jer 31:31–33.
18. Ez 36:26.

Vastly more than a law or an added burden, the Gospel is a grace, an outpouring of mercy, a promise of interior transformation by the Holy Spirit. As St. Paul tells us, "*For I am not ashamed of the gospel: it is the power of God for salvation to every one who has faith, to the Jew first and also to the Greek.*"[19]

So there is an absolutely essential relationship: between Beatitudes and Holy Spirit and mission. Theologians of the Middle Ages like St. Thomas Aquinas, following St. Augustine, pointed to the link between the Beatitudes and the seven gifts of the Spirit. This may seem a little artificial at first, but the intuition is sound. In living the Beatitudes we are open to the gifts of the Spirit, while, inversely, only the Holy Spirit can give us the understanding to practice the Beatitudes fully.

We can consider the Beatitudes one by one and show how they require this work by the Holy Spirit, who alone can make the human heart capable of understanding and living them. Poverty, meekness, tears, the hunger and thirst for God, mercy, purity of heart, fostering peace, joy in persecution—all presuppose a heart transformed by the Spirit.

---

19. Rom 1:16.

We can also consider how the Beatitudes point to difficult situations that are opportunities in that they provide an opportunity for an outpouring of the Holy Spirit, who transforms suffering by disclosing in it the presence of God and God's Kingdom.

This is one of the fundamental keys to reading this Gospel text. The happiness promised by the Beatitudes is not simply a human happiness or satisfaction, but a visitation of the Holy Spirit, a divine consolation. The Holy Spirit is drawn to the situations and attitudes described by the Beatitudes. The Holy Spirit comes to rest in a special way on one who is poor in spirit, meek, humble, suffering, merciful, and persecuted. Suddenly, in situations where no happiness can be seen and no satisfaction is sought, there is the surprising gift of happiness—a free gift of the Holy Spirit, the consoler, which descends gently upon one. St. Peter speaks of this in his first letter when he says of persecutions: "*If you are reproached for the name of Christ, you are blessed, because the spirit of glory and of God rests upon you.*"[20] But we could show that each of the eight Beatitudes describes a situation

---

20. 1 Pt 4:14.

or attitude that prompts an effusion of the Spirit on human weakness, an eruption of grace in the life of the person involved.

Thus the Beatitudes describe the conditions necessary for a person to be fully open to the Spirit's action: in faithfully following the path outlined by the Beatitudes, he or she is open to the work of the Spirit. The fundamental question of Christian life is how to make oneself fully open to the Spirit and the action of divine grace. We can accomplish nothing by ourselves. Only the work of the Spirit can transform us and enable us to fulfill our vocations. "*It is the spirit that gives life, the flesh is of no avail.*"[21] From this perspective, the Gospel of the Beatitudes is Jesus' response to the question of how we receive the Holy Spirit.

We can say, then, that the Beatitudes are both fruits of the Holy Spirit and conditions for receiving the Spirit. This is no contradiction. It expresses the circularity proper to the spiritual domain and the mysterious interaction between divine grace and human agency.

---

21. Jn 6:63.

THE BEATITUDES, THE WAY OF HUMAN MATURITY

The Beatitudes, one might say, are not only the most profound revelation of the mystery of God but also a complete treatise on spiritual life. They show what we are called to be as Christians, what it really means to live the Gospel. They describe true human and spiritual maturity. A portrait of Christ, they are also the portrait of the mature Christian in Christ, a son or daughter of the Father who is free in the Spirit. They sum up the most perfect realization of human existence. A pathway to humanization, they are also a way of fruitfulness, showing us how to bear fruit that lasts, how to spread love and inspire others to true life.

While doing some teaching on spiritual fatherhood for priests, one of my fundamental points was that a priest manifests the beautiful grace of fatherhood at work to the extent that he becomes a man of the Beatitudes. This principle applies to all fatherhood and motherhood in the Church, and to fruitfulness in general. A life lived according to the Beatitudes is a life that is beautiful and fruitful.

The Gospel isn't a legal code superimposed on life (and perhaps making it more difficult or complicated).

Rather, it discloses the fundamental laws of existence and describes the conditions that make authentic, free, and fruitful love possible. Embracing the Gospel means going directly to the roots—to the simplicity and unity of life, by uncovering its ultimate meaning and understanding the conditions of true happiness.

Coherence and Unity

The Beatitudes are intrinsically interrelated. Probing deeply into any one of them leads to the others. Nor can we truly live one without living all. They are inseparable, indissoluble.

While each one of them has its own specific nature and value, the person described by each phrase (poor, meek, merciful, etc.) is always the same person: a disciple of Jesus, considered in different aspects of his or her life.

Similarly, the reward announced (inheriting the Kingdom, being consoled, being called children of God, etc.) is always the same, considered in different ways. It is always access to the Kingdom, entry into the richness of the mystery of God, in its different manifestations. In meditating on the Beatitudes, it is good to contemplate the particular grace each offers: inheriting the Kingdom, being consoled, inheriting the earth, being satisfied, obtaining mercy, seeing God, being called children of God. What more is there to desire? This should give us that joy and happiness promised at the end.

The profound unity of the Beatitudes and the need to embrace them all is no obstacle to each Christian having his or her personal, unique way of living them out. There is a particular entrance to the mystery of the one true Kingdom for each of us. According to our personal vocations, and as a function of the various stages of our lives, we are called to live one or another of the Beatitudes more fully. This is easily seen in the lives of saints and Christians generally.

Let us pray, then, that God enlighten us concerning which Beatitude should be the focus of our lives here and now—which, that is, will be most helpful to us at the present stage of our spiritual struggle. I hope this book sheds some light on that for its readers.

Personal and Community Aspects of the Beatitudes

The Beatitudes are a call to personal conversion, an interior transformation that first concerns the individual.

But they also have a community dimension that isn't always discussed enough. They speak of what make any life possible, since without humility, mercy, meekness, and the rest no community can survive.

Furthermore, they can't really be truly lived except with a community (how can you be poor apart from relation to another, how do you practice meekness or patience or humility without close partners in life?). Community life is the essential place for living them, for having a concrete experience of their truth and fruitfulness.

Many religious communities and Gospel movements not surprisingly refer to the Beatitudes in their rules. And there is much to be said for couples and families as congenial to understanding and practicing them. The family is the first and most essential of all Christian communities. Where can we better experience our own poverty and that of others than in the closely shared life of a couple and family members?

The meaning, beauty, and radiance of the Beatitudes are fully realized in the rule of community life. The "poor of the Lord" (a scriptural expression we'll return to) have always felt a need to be together, to live as brothers and sisters, to encourage one another mutually, to share, to join in celebrating the love and faithfulness of the Lord. They recognize one another at first glance, feel themselves members of the same spiritual family. Consider such historical examples as the pious groups of *Anawim* in the history of Israel (whose piety, hope, and interior attitudes are often reflected in the Psalms), the Church in Jerusalem as it is described in the Acts of the Apostles, the Franciscan movement in its early days, and some of the new communities inspired by the Holy Spirit in today's Church.

The Church has always had privileged places for witnessing in a visible and instructive way the splendor of this Gospel message. Let's hope there will be even more. And since this vocation rests in a particular way today on families, let's also hope many families hear this call more clearly than ever and model themselves on this Gospel ideal instead of the spirit of the world.

PRESENT REALITY AND ESCHATOLOGICAL FULFILLMENT

The Beatitudes have an obvious eschatological aspect. The happiness they promise will not be fully experienced until we enter the Kingdom of God. On earth we have only a partial participation, a foretaste. At the same time, though, the Kingdom is already present.

Following the path traced by the Beatitudes with determination and faithfulness, we will surely experience their profound truth and enjoy part of the happiness they promise. Not yet in the light and in full possession, we go forward in faith and hope. But if we advance with full sincerity, we will not lack the consolation of the Holy Spirit and a down payment, as it were, of the inheritance promised us—partial yet sufficiently real and solid to be strong encouragement to persevere in living according to the wisdom of the Gospel.

Now we shall look at each of the Beatitudes in the order in which the Gospel of Matthew lists them. We shall dwell at length on the first, the Beatitude of the poor in spirit, seeking to understand the crucial theme of spiritual poverty. Then, having already spoken of some aspects of the other Beatitudes, we shall return to each in its turn.

THE POOR IN SPIRIT

The *only good* is to love God with all one's heart and to
be *poor in spirit* here on earth.
—THÉRÈSE OF LISIEUX[1]

We experience such great peace when we're totally poor,
when we depend upon no one except God.
—THÉRÈSE OF LISIEUX[2]

Do not fear, the poorer you are the more Jesus will love you.
—THÉRÈSE OF LISIEUX[3]

The first of the Beatitudes proclaimed by Jesus is
"Blessed are the poor in spirit, for theirs is the kingdom of

---

1. *Story of a Soul: The Autobiography of St. Thérèse of Lisieux,* trans.
John Clarke, OCD (Washington, D.C.: ICS Publications, 1996), loc.
1601 of 6450, Kindle.

2. Thérèse of Lisieux, *St. Thérèse of Lisieux: Her Last Conversations,* trans.
John Clarke, OCD (Washington, D.C.: ICS Publications, 1977), Aug. 6.4.

3. Thérèse of Lisieux, *General Correspondence Volume Two*, trans. John
Clarke, OCD (Washington, D.C.: ICS Publications, 1988), LT 211.

heaven." The Greek text reads "*ptochos to pneuma,*" poor in the spirit, but this sometimes is translated "happy are those who have the heart of a poor one" and "happy are those with the soul of a poor one."

This first Beatitude is the source of all the others; it contains them all, as a seed contains a plant. One could easily show how each following Beatitude presupposes some form of poorness of heart. At the heart of the Gospel and of the person of Christ is a mystery of poverty. This is the absolutely essential key to grasping the Christian logic as St. Paul expresses it. "*For you know the grace of our Lord Jesus Christ, that though he was rich, yet for your sake he became poor, so that by his poverty you might become rich.*"[4]

Still, this isn't easy to understand. Even in the spiritual realm we tend to think in terms of riches, of the acquisition and accumulation of certain goods. It takes time and experience to realize the profound truth of this text. But I am increasingly persuaded that spiritual poverty is the key to the spiritual life, to holiness, to fruitfulness, as well as true happiness. Only the poor fully receive the grace of the Holy Spirit, the revelation of the mystery of God, as Jesus says in the Gospel of Luke:

---

4. 2 Cor 8:9.

In that same hour he rejoiced in the Holy Spirit and said, "I thank thee, Father, Lord of heaven and earth, that thou hast hidden these things from the wise and understanding and revealed them to babes; yea, Father, for such was thy gracious will."[5]

Yes, there is such a thing as a negative poverty (material or moral bankruptcy, interior emptiness), and of course we must fight against it, as the Church has always done. But there is also a good poverty, source of life and joy, to which Jesus invites us and the saints give witness. "*There is no joy comparable to that which the truly poor in spirit experience,*" says Thérèse of Lisieux.[6]

What does this spiritual poverty consist of? If I had to sum it up in one sentence, I would say it is essentially a form of freedom, *the freedom to receive everything freely and to give everything freely.*

When Jesus sends his apostles out, he tells them: "*And preach as you go, saying, 'The kingdom of heaven is at hand.' Heal the sick, raise the dead, cleanse lepers, cast out demons. You received without pay, give without pay.*"[7]

The most striking thing about the disciples' mission is its material precariousness: they are to rely only

---

5. Lk 10:21.

6. Thérèse of Lisieux, *Story of a Soul*, loc. 3949 of 6540.

7. Mt 10:7–8.

on God and, in doing so, experience his providential care. And at the same time, he promises them a powerful grace: the grace of healing, authority over the powers of evil, the capacity to spread peace. The power of the Spirit will rest on their poverty.

It seems to me that the words "*You received without paying, give without pay*" are of critical importance. They seem to sum up the essence of Christian life, of living by the logic of the Kingdom. Here is what Jesus calls the "justice of the Kingdom," as he says, "*But seek first his kingdom and his righteousness, and all these things shall be yours as well.*"[8]

On the one hand, this logic means receiving everything freely from the love and mercy of God, not just what we deserve or according to some "right" we might claim, but also according to the rich generosity of his kindness. It means understanding that God's gifts are not to be seized but received. On the other hand, it means giving all we have received, sharing it with the same generosity and freedom with which God gave it to us.

Poverty of heart, then, is really the freedom that is present in receiving everything freely and of giving everything freely, setting aside ego, with its pretensions

---

8. Mt 6:33.

and demands. It means dying to self, a radical detachment that leads us to the perfect transparency of God's actions, and to the joy of receiving and giving freely.

But it requires a long time and much work to attain this freedom. We must undergo a profound transformation in our way of relating to God, to ourselves, and to others.

Poverty in the Old Testament

To understand the meaning of poverty of spirit really well and learn how to achieve it little by little, let's start by examining the roots of this notion in the Old Testament. In preaching the Beatitudes, Jesus shows the newness of the Gospel, but the ground is laid for this newness in the history of Israel. Thus the message of the Beatitudes, and especially of poverty, cannot be understood apart from the gradual emergence of a positive view of poverty in the Old Testament. This will help us see how to practice poverty and what it means to be poor in relation to God, ourselves, and others—the whole of life, in other words.

The Old Testament discusses poverty from various complex perspectives, not all of which we can examine here. At the most primitive level, poverty is often seen as a negative reality, even a sign of divine punishment, while wealth is viewed as God's blessing. In other passages, especially some of the prophets, poverty is considered a scandal, an atrocious injustice when it occurs in Israel, and so there are vigorous appeals to remedy all sorts of social injustice, to care for the poor and foreigners, and so on.

These passages remain relevant, of course. The polemic against the egotistical and indifferent rich occur again in the New Testament and the Gospel itself (for instance, the parable of the Rich Man and Lazarus[9]) together with pleading on behalf of the poor. Recall the fearsome words of St. James:

> Come now, you rich, weep and howl for the miseries that are coming upon you. Your riches have rotted and your garments are moth-eaten. Your gold and silver have rusted, and their rust will be evidence against you and will eat your flesh like fire. You have laid up treasure for the last days. Behold, the wages of the laborers who mowed your fields, which you kept back by fraud, cry out; and the cries of the harvesters have reached the ears of the Lord of hosts.[10]

---

9. Lk 16:19–31.
10. Jas 5:1–4.

How timely these words are in today's world, where the inequality between rich and poor grows and grows, where injustice arising from love of money is so common, and where the blood of the poor cries out to God!

At the moment, though, we are concerned with the Old Testament, especially the texts mirroring the destruction of Jerusalem and the Babylonian exile. Here we find a positive view of poverty emerging—what one might call a spirituality of poverty— along with the figure of "the poor of the Lord." It can be seen in several of the prophets, particularly the second half of the book of Isaiah, in some of the Wisdom books, and especially in the Psalms, where this theme is very frequent.

These passages contain a constellation of terms associated with the idea of poverty: poor, weak, little, humble, afflicted, oppressed, indigent, famished, unfortunate, broken-hearted. We also encounter certain social situations characterized by insecurity: widow, orphan, foreigner. We find descriptions of factual situations (difficult or humiliating social situations, distress, conflicts) and also of interior dispositions (humility, meekness, simplicity, hope in God, etc.).

At the same time, the fundamental idea—or, more precisely, the spiritual insight to which Scripture testifies—seems fairly simple. What is a poor person in the Old Testament? He or she is someone in a situation that is sorrowful, suffering, precarious, humiliating, or something similar, who, because of the situation, can no longer count on anyone but God. Lacking any help or support on this earth, preyed upon by distress, often the object of the disdain of the rich and powerful, the person has only one last recourse: to cry out to the Lord. "*Be not far from me, for trouble is near and there is none to help.*"[11] Yet, by this very fact, he or she eventually will experience God's goodness and faithfulness toward those who count on him.

From the very start, then, we see a sorrowful and negative reality transformed into something extremely positive. All the richness of God's mercy, goodness, and tenderness are in the end extended to this poor person, so that he or she comes to enjoy true knowledge of God. No longer a vague or abstract idea, God is known as living and merciful, the God of tenderness and pity of whom the Psalms sing.

All this, however, supposes that poverty is not just a factual condition but a state that little by little evokes an interior attitude of humility, littleness, and openness to God, of confident hope in his mercy.

---

11. Ps 22:11.

Poverty like this is often linked to material conditions, but not always. Scripture contains beautiful instances of the poverty of rich people in the sense described here. One of these is David, who according to biblical tradition gradually became a great example of interior poverty through his repentance after sinning,[12] and also through his distress: exiled from Jerusalem by the revolt of his son Absalom, he climbs the Mount of Olives weeping.[13]

The prayer of Queen Esther is another good example. Her situation is not material poverty, but internal anguish and suffering. Meaning to exterminate the Jews, Amman mounts a persecution against them. The queen, unable to remain silent in the face of this threat to her people, determines to intercede with the king and, risking her life, goes to him. The law made anyone approaching the king uninvited liable to death. Before acting, Esther fasts, does penance, and begs God:

> O my Lord, thou only art our King; help me, who am alone and have no helper but thee, for my danger is in my hand. . . . Oh God, whose might is over all, hear the voice of the despairing, and save

---

12. 2 Sm 11 and 12.
13. 2 Sm 15:30.

us from the hands of evildoers. And save me from my fear![14]

The poor person has no support, no human security. But if he turns to God, God will be his refuge and his comfort.

The Tenderness of God for the Poor

One of the Old Testament's most frequent affirmations, particularly in the Psalms, concerns the tenderness God has for the poor who count on him. Let's look at some examples, not only reading them but keeping them in our hearts as expressions of God's goodness and faithfulness toward humankind.

In the second half of Isaiah we find these passages:

Fear not, you worm Jacob, you men of Israel! I will help you, says the LORD; your Redeemer is the Holy One of Israel.[15]

Sing for joy, O heavens, and exult, O earth; break forth, O mountains, into singing! For the LORD has comforted his people, and will have compassion on his afflicted. But Zion said, "The LORD has forsaken

---

14. Est 14: 3b-4; 19.
15. Is 41:14.

me, my Lord has forgotten me." "Can a woman forget her sucking child, that she should have no compassion on the son of her womb? Even these may forget, yet I will not forget you. Behold, I have graven you on the palms of my hands. . . ."[16]

I dwell in the high and holy place, and also with him who is of a contrite and humble spirit, to revive the spirit of the humble, and to revive the heart of the contrite.[17]

Thus says the Lord: "Heaven is my throne and the earth is my footstool; what is the house which you would build for me, and what is the place of my rest? All these things my hand has made, and so all these things are mine, says the Lord. But this is the man to whom I will look, he that is humble and contrite in spirit, and trembles at my word."[18]

Here are some passages from the Psalms:

For the needy shall not always be forgotten, and the hope of the poor shall not perish for ever.[19]

---

16. Is 49:13–16.
17. Is 57:15.
18. Is 66:1–2.
19. Ps 9:18.

For he has not despised or abhorred the affliction of the afflicted; and he has not hid his face from him, but has heard, when he cried to him.[20]

He leads the humble in what is right, and teaches the humble his way.[21]

This poor man cried, and the LORD heard him, and saved him out of all his troubles.[22]

The LORD is near to the brokenhearted, and saves the crushed in spirit.[23]

I am poor and needy; but the LORD takes thought for me.[24]

He raises the poor from the dust, and lifts the needy form the ash heap, to make them sit with princes, with the princes of his people.[25]

The LORD preserves the simple; when I was brought low, he saved me.[26]

---

20. Ps 22:24, Psalm of the Passion.

21. Ps 25:9.

22. Ps 34:6.

23. Ps 34:18.

24. Ps 40:17.

25. Ps 113:7–8.

26. Ps 116:6.

One of the fundamental ideas of Scripture is that in the Messianic age the poor will be honored. There will be a reversal of situations: those who were humbled or excluded will be in the highest place. Here is an example from Isaiah:

> In that day the deaf shall hear the words of a book, and out of their gloom and darkness the eyes of the blind shall see. The meek shall obtain fresh joy in the LORD, and the poor among men shall exult in the Holy One of Israel.[27]

And this is how Psalm 71 describes the ideal king of whom Israel dreams:

> May he defend the cause of the poor of the people, give deliverance to the needy, and crush the oppressor! . . . For he delivers the needy when he calls, the poor and him who has no helper. He has pity on the weak and the needy, and saves the lives of the needy.[28]

Mary sings of this reversal in the Messianic age in her *Magnificat*. "*He has put down the mighty from their thrones, and exalted those of low degree.*"[29]

---

27. Is 29:18–19.
28. Ps 71:4, 12–13.
29. Lk 1:52.

THE TEST OF TIME

But God's intervention on behalf of the poor isn't always immediate, and this can cause difficulties. The promises of the Beatitudes sometimes seem contradicted by reality. So many poor people seem to be forgotten, so many weep and are not consoled, so many are hungry or thirsty for justice and not satisfied!

Yet God is faithful, all his promises will be fulfilled. Not an iota of the law will be forgotten, as Jesus affirms.

Sometimes there are mysterious delays before God's intervention on behalf of the poor occurs. God's apparent silence tests endurance. The cry repeated in several Psalms is, "*How long?*"

> How long, O LORD? Wilt thou forget me for ever?
> How long wilt thou hide thy face from me?
> How long must I bear pain in my soul, and have
>   sorrow in my heart all the day?
> How long shall my enemy be exalted over me?
> Consider and answer me, O LORD my God![30]

But notice that this sorrowful questioning concludes with an act of hope: "*But I have trusted in thy*

---

30. Ps 13:1–3.

steadfast love; my heart shall rejoice in thy salvation. I will sing to the Lord, because he has dealt bountifully with me."[31]

We find similar passages elsewhere, for example, Psalm 42:

> I say to God, my rock: "Why hast thou forgotten me? Why go I mourning because of the oppression of the enemy? . . .
>
> Why are you cast down, O my soul, and why are you disquieted within me? Hope in God; for I shall again praise him, my help and my God.[32]

God's response is certain, but it can't be foreseen or programmed. Patience and sorrow have their place, but in the end even they are positive in that they perform a hidden work, create a desire, prepare an interior space for embracing the compensatory reward when it finally comes. "*It is good that one should wait quietly for the salvation of the LORD.*"[33] God's response will be so much more beautiful and rich when the wait has been long and trying.

---

31. Ps 13:5–6.
32. Ps 42:9, 11.
33. Lam 3:26.

Among other things, interior poverty leads us to consent to the experience of not being masters of our time, unable to manipulate God or oblige him to enter into our expectations or plans. His intervention remains free and sovereign, unforeseen. Having mastery of a time frame carries with it enormous human security and makes waiting easier. But there is no time frame into which God can be forced. "*You know neither the day nor the hour,*" Jesus says.[34]

The poverty of not being masters of our own time is hard to bear, but it calls us to a purer hope, one without human support. Little by little it engenders patience, humility, meekness, creating the desire that one day will bring fulfillment beyond all expectations.

POVERTY AS A TRIAL AND A GRACE. THE EXPERIENCE OF THE DESERT

One of the most essential Old Testament texts for understanding the meaning of spiritual poverty is chapter 8 of Deuteronomy. It contains a fragment of a long discourse by Moses to the people, a magnificent synthesis of what we might call "the experience of the

---

34. Mt 25:13.

desert." For Israel the forty years of wandering after leaving Egypt and before entering the Promised Land were a foundational experience, but they symbolize a reality that is part of any spiritual journey.

> And you shall remember all the way which the LORD your God has led you these forty years in the wilderness, that he might humble you, testing you to know what was in your heart, whether you would keep his commandments, or not. And he humbled you and let you hunger and fed you with manna, which you did not know, nor did your fathers know; that he might make you know that man does not live by bread alone, but that man lives by everything that proceeds out of the mouth of the LORD. Your clothing did not wear out upon you, and your foot did not swell, these forty years. Know then in your heart that, as a man disciplines his son, the LORD your God disciplines you.[35]

The Lord wished to have Israel, like each of us, pass through a paradoxical experience, a sorrowful path of poverty, of humiliation that was at the same time a wonderful experience of faithfulness to his providence.

---

35. Dt 8:2–5.

God nourished his people with manna, their clothes were not worn out, their feet were not swollen.

The experience of poverty is meant to help us realize what we truly have in our hearts, to know ourselves as we are, without illusions. It is meant also to awaken a new hunger in our hearts, hunger for God. In poverty, at the heart of the struggle, we realize that no food, no satisfaction, and no human security can suffice. We must direct our desires toward God.

When we do that, the Lord reveals himself and gives us an entirely new, previously unknown food: manna, the food that comes from the very mouth of God, the words of truth and of love he addresses to his children, the breath from the divine mouth that discreetly sustains us. This trial is a time of humiliation but also of grace, for it makes us open up to new nourishment, new resources to which we were not accustomed before—a nourishment that is not physical, much more subtle, but the only one that can make us stronger. No longer Egypt's cauldrons of meat and its bread but a delicate dew, not to be kept for tomorrow but given each day by the Lord, in just the amount each one needs, neither more nor less.[36] Here is the nourishment that makes it

---

36. See Chapter 16 of Exodus.

possible for the people to make the long journey to the Promised Land.

God gives himself as food to the poor person who counts on him. This beautiful mystery reaches its supreme fulfillment in the Eucharist. And to fully appreciate the Eucharist and to receive its riches, one needs a poor heart.

POVERTY, HUMILITY, MEEKNESS

The Hebrew Bible uses several terms to express the idea of poverty. The most important is *anav* (*anawim* in the plural). Depending on the context, it means "poor" or "humble" or "meek," and all three of these can be found in our modern Bibles as well as in the ancient Greek translations of the Hebrew Bible. And it is a matter of profound significance that these terms are also found in the Beatitudes and other New Testament passages.

The book of Numbers uses the word *anav* in an interesting passage about Moses. After the exodus, he was accompanied by his brother Aaron and his sister Miriam, but their relationship was strained because of a marriage of which Aaron and Miriam did not approve.

> Miriam and Aaron spoke against Moses because of the Cushite woman whom he had married, for he had

married a Cushite woman; and they said, "Has the LORD indeed spoken only through Moses? Has he not spoken through us also?" And the LORD heard it. Now the man Moses was very meek, more than all men that were on the face of the earth. And suddenly the LORD said to Moses and to Aaron and Miriam, "Come out, you three, to the tent of meeting." And the three of them came out. And the LORD came down in a pillar of cloud, and stood at the door of the tent, and called Aaron and Miriam; and they both came forward. And he said, "Hear my words: If there is a prophet among you, I the LORD make myself known to him in a vision, I speak with him in a dream. Not so with my servant Moses; he is entrusted with all my house. With him I speak mouth to mouth, clearly, and not in dark speech; and he beholds the form of the LORD. Why then were you not afraid to speak against my servant Moses?"

And the anger of the LORD was kindled against them, and he departed; and when the cloud removed from over the tent, behold, Miriam was leprous, as white as snow. And Aaron turned towards Miriam and behold, she was leprous. And Aaron said to Moses, "Oh, my lord, do not punish us because we have done foolishly and have sinned. Let her not be as one dead, of whom the flesh is half consumed when he comes out of his mother's womb." And Moses cried to the LORD, "Heal her, O God, I beseech thee." But the Lord said to Moses, "If her father had but spit in her face, should she not be shamed seven days? Let her be shut up outside the camp seven days, and after that she may be brought in again." So Miriam was shut up outside the camp seven days.[37]

We don't know why Moses' brother and sister objected to his marriage, but this episode is an occasion for the venting of a different grievance, deeper and no doubt latent for a long time—namely, a certain jealousy toward Moses. But why speak only of these people? Is not the Lord speaking also to us?

Moses' meekness and humility, faced with this criticism and bitterness, are described in a beautiful way: "a man more meek than all men that were on the face of the earth" (or, it might be rendered, more humble). He is not angry or defensive, and remains silent. Then God himself intervenes to defend his servant and punish Miriam by making her a leper. Yet, Moses prays that his sister may be healed! God, who can refuse nothing to his servant, does so, while keeping her outside the camp for seven days to have time to reflect a bit on her conduct.

---

37. Nm 12:1–15.

God's words show how unique was the relationship between him and Moses, a bond closer than that with any other prophet. God entrusted his people to Moses, spoke with him face to face. For Moses was so humble, so poor of heart, that God entered into intimacy with him and confided so many things to him.

How Do We Become the Most Humble on Earth?

The characterization of Moses as the humblest man on earth is a prefiguration of Christ. It has two sources.

There is a humility that comes from suffering, from trials, in which we experience our limits, our weakness, and become progressively humble. This is absolutely necessary: as Bernadette of Lourdes said: "*Many humiliations are necessary to create a little humility!*" We should be deeply grateful to the Lord for the situations we experience that impoverish us, humiliate us, make us realize our weakness and our misery. Thérèse of Lisieux said: "*The Almighty has done great things in the soul of his divine mother's child, and the greatest thing is to have shown her her* littleness, *her impotence.*"[38] One part of Moses' humility had this source.

---

38. Thérèse of Lisieux, *Story of a Soul*, loc. 3646 of 6450.

But there is another source of humility, far deeper and radical: the experience of God. Moses was so humble, more than all the others, because his experience of God was so much deeper: did he not spend forty days and nights on Mount Sinai speaking with God in the clouds?

It might be said that there is a "lower form of poverty" and a "higher form of poverty." One comes from human experience, the other from the austerity, much more radical, that the Holy Spirit works within us.

"*Happy is the soul that possesses this celestial blessing, that is poor in spirit by the Spirit of God, which grace has made poor and not the trials and coercion of life's misfortunes!*" declared Catherine de Bar, seventeenth-century founder of a religious community.[39]

This is what the saints experience in those spiritual "nights" they sometimes go through. Without using this language, which is often poorly understood, we can simply say an encounter with God, especially in authentic prayer, necessarily involves sorrowful elements. Similarly, there is no way to have real interior poverty without great faithfulness to prayer, the truth–bearing activity in which human beings stand radically

---

39. Catherine Mectilde de Bar, *Adorer et adhérer* (Paris: Éditions du Cerf, 1994), p. 109.

poor and naked before God. Teresa of Avila says in *The Interior Castle*: "*It's in contemplating his greatness that we discover our lowliness, in seeing his purity that we see our dirtiness, in considering his humility that we see how far we are from being humble.*" The first step in acquiring humility is to recognize that we have none.

The deeper our encounter with God, the more humble we become. Humility is a sign of a real experience of God. Such an encounter with the living God destroys all pride: in knowing God in his power and majesty, we understand that we are nothing compared to him. Our limits are revealed, our sin and radical poverty are disclosed. The implacable purity of the divine light, like a ray of sunshine piercing a dark room and showing the tiniest specks of dust, gives the soul evidence of its misery and absolute incapacity.[40] We see this clearly in Scripture. Job,

---

40. See this related passage from Teresa of Avila: "*When the prayer comes from God's spirit, there is no need to go dredging up things in order to derive some humility and shame because the Lord Himself gives this prayer in a manner very different from that which we gain through our nice little reasonings. For such humility is nothing in comparison with the true humility the Lord with His light here teaches and which causes an embarrassment that undoes one. It is well known that God gives a knowledge that makes us realize we have no good of ourselves; and the greater the favors, the greater is this knowledge*" (Teresa of Avila, *The Book of Her Life*, trans. Kieran Kavanaugh and Otilio Rodriguez, OCD (Indianapolis: Hackett, 2008), 94).

after God spoke to him, is aware that he must be silent: "*I had heard of thee by the hearing of the ear, but now my eye sees thee; therefore I despise myself, and repent in dust and ashes.*"[41] Isaiah, having seen God in the sanctuary borne upon clouds and surrounded by seraphim whose voices proclaim the divine holiness and make the gateposts shake, exclaims: "*Woe is me! For I am lost; for I am a man of unclean lips.*"[42] Peter, after the miraculous catch of fish, throws himself at Jesus' feet, saying, "*Depart from me, for I am a sinful man, O Lord!*"[43]

Human beings discover the extraordinary humility of God insofar as they deepen their encounter with God, who humbled himself to experience human weakness.[44] Only God is truly humble, only God is capable of humbling himself, as we see in the mystery of Christ. From what height could humankind lower itself? There is no real humility except by participating in divine humility, which is revealed to us so perfectly in Christ, especially in his obedience and humiliation on the Cross.

---

41. Jb 42:5–6.

42. Is 6:5.

43. Lk 5:8.

44. Cf. Phil 2:5–8.

True humility is not a human invention. We are all capable of false modesty. We must, as St. Paul says, put on the humility of Christ.[45]

The same can be said for meekness, one of humility's most beautiful fruits (as opposed to hardness, a fruit of pride). Only God is meek, and all true meekness is a participation in divine meekness. The source of all humility and all meekness is the heart of Christ, as Christ's words in Matthew's gospel attests: "*Take my yoke upon you, and learn from me; for I am gentle and lowly in heart, and you will find rest for your souls.*"[46]

An experience of God, and therefore of faith, contains an intrinsic note of humility. Faith presupposes receptiveness, docility, and obedience, which only a humble person is capable of. True faith has no arrogance, as Pope Francis says in the encyclical *Lumen Fidei*. A person with authentic Christian faith is always acutely aware that this is a free gift, not something of which he or she can be proud of.

> As a truth of love, it is not one that can be imposed
> by force; it is not a truth that stifles the individual.
> Since it is born of love, it can penetrate to the heart,

---

45. Cf. Phil 2:4–6.
46. Mt 11:29.

to the personal core of each man and woman. Clearly,
then, faith is not intransigent, but grows in respect-
ful coexistence with others. One who believes may
not be presumptuous; on the contrary, truth leads
to humility, since believers know that, rather than
ourselves possessing truth, it is truth which embraces
and possesses us. Far from making us inflexible, the
security of faith sets us on a journey; it enables witness and dialogue with all.[47]

Genuine love also is humble. Someone deeply in
love—especially when the love is reciprocated—always
has the feeling that this love is a kind of grace, a gift,
not a personal achievement to the glory in.

Humility is essential because it is both sign and
condition of all authentic love. To love is to leave
behind any pretension of self-sufficiency, all arrogance,
all domination, all possessiveness, all superiority, while
making oneself small before the other and embracing
the other in his or her poverty and weakness. No love is
true and durable except that between two poor hearts.
The rich are forever in competition. Only the poor of
heart know how to love and embrace each other recip-
rocally. God made himself poor because he is love.

47. Francis, Encyclical *Lumen Fidei* (June 29, 2013), 34.

The Poor Who Remain in Israel

Returning to our exploration of the meaning of spiritual poverty in the Old Testament and of the word *anaw*, which specifically describes it, let us now take a look at another passage, a very different one, in which the mystery of poverty is central. It is from Zephaniah, a prophet of the seventh century before Christ.

As in many of the prophetic books Zephaniah begins with an invitation to conversion, then looks at the future, announcing God's intervention, and concludes with magnificent promises of Jerusalem's restoration. But that will be only after a period of sorrowful humiliations and purifications such as Isaiah speaks of when writing about the Israelites who remain faithful.

The conversion to which the prophet invites us is essentially the elimination of all pride. "*Seek the Lord, all you humble of the land, who do his commands; seek righteousness, seek humility; perhaps you may be hidden on the day of the wrath of the Lord.*"[48]

---

48. Zep 2:3.

Later, in a very important passage, Zephaniah sees the people of the future, the renewed Israel, as a people of poverty:

> On that day you shall not be put to shame because of the deeds by which you have rebelled against me; for then I will remove from your midst your proudly exultant ones, and you shall no longer be haughty in my holy mountain.
>
> For I will leave in the midst of you a people humble and lowly. They shall seek refuge in the name of the LORD, those who are left in Israel; they shall do no wrong and utter no lies, nor shall there be found in their mouth a deceitful tongue. For they shall pasture and lie down, and none shall make them afraid.[49]

Israel will be healed of its sin and its offenses against God, freed from all shame, and this healing will be essentially a purification from all pride, from all human pretension. Here is one of the fundamental themes of Isaiah's prediction:

> For the LORD of hosts has a day against all that is proud and lofty, against all that is lifted up and high. . . . And the haughtiness of man shall be

---

49. Zep 3:11–13.

humbled, and the pride of men shall be brought low;
and the LORD alone will be exalted in that day. And
the idols shall utterly pass away.[50]

This purification will be radical, and God will let
only "*meek and lowly people*" remain in Israel (*ani* and
dal, poor and weak, or without importance).

The fruits of this purification will be very positive:
"those who are left" will find *refuge* in the name of the
Lord. God will be their power and their refuge, their
unshakable security. This little people will be rooted
in *truth*: no more lies, no more deceit. All will be completely truthful with God, with themselves, with others.

They will *graze*: God himself will give them the
nourishment they need. Finally, they will *lie down and
none shall make them afraid*. They will be at peace, rest-
ing in God, they will have no more fear or worry.

The prophet is thus announcing that a time of radical poverty will come, but one with very positive ben-
efits: holiness, truth, freedom, security, peace, interior
power. The poor will find all they need in God.

This text describes God's pedagogy toward Israel.
God permits trials, sorrowful humiliations and severe
losses, to form "those who are left," and from this just

---

50. Is 2:12–18.

people the Messiah will be born. We encounter this just people at the beginning of the New Testament, personified in Mary. The rest of Zephaniah's text, the magnificent promises of salvation, is used often by the liturgy in speaking about the Virgin:

> Sing aloud, O daughter of Zion; shout, O Israel! Rejoice and exult with all your heart, O daughter of Jerusalem!
>
> The Lord has taken away the judgments against you, he has cast out your enemies. The King of Israel, the Lord, is in your midst; you shall fear evil no more.
>
> On that day it shall be said to Jerusalem: "Do not fear, O Zion; let not your hands grow weak.
>
> The Lord, your God, is in your midst, a warrior who gives victory; he will rejoice over you with gladness, he will renew you in his love; he will exult over you with loud singing as on a day of festival."[51]

This does not apply only to Israel, but to the Church in general. We are not better than our fathers. Obviously, not all the tribulations in the Church's history are found here, but there are certainly periods of

---

51. Zep 3:14–18.

humiliation and sorrowful purification in the history of ecclesiastical communities that make them poor and humble, mirroring the Beatitudes. Trials are a necessary part of the experience of every community and person.

Zephaniah's text also expresses God's pedagogy toward each believer. The destruction of all pride, all arrogance, all pretensions and human illusions, is part, though not the whole, of every spiritual itinerary. "*No human being might boast in the presence of God*," says Paul.[52] The words of the prophet can be taken as God's words addressed personally to each of us: I will eradicate from you all pride and you will cease being proud, permitting you only a humble and poor heart, and only then will you find your refuge in God, your truth, your nourishment, your power, and your peace.

Spiritual poverty must touch all aspects of our lives. It is helpful to see how this is expressed in our fundamental relationships: with God, with self, with others, and finally with the world in general. Being poor in spirit in all these relationships is a source of freedom and of joy.

---

52. 1 Cor 1:29.

Poverty in the Relationship with God

Poverty means first of all being truthful toward God: realizing our radical limitations as creatures, our total dependence on his love. It also means recognizing our condition as sinners who so badly need his mercy and pardon so much. "*If thou, O Lord, shouldst mark iniquities, Lord, who could stand?*"[53]

This realization brings about humility and repentance, but never sadness or discouragement. Hope in infinite mercy must always accompany one's consciousness of sin, for without this hope we have not entered into the fullness of truth. God's love will always be greater than our faults. "*O Israel, hope in the Lord! For with the Lord there is steadfast love, and with him is plenteous redemption.*"[54] He who sees himself as poor is the special object of God's love: "*But this is the man to whom I will look, he that is humble and contrite in spirit, and trembles at my word.*"[55]

To be poor in relation to God means recognizing that everything is given us as a free gift of his mercy. All

---

53. Ps 130:3
54. Ps 130:7.
55. Is 66:2.

we are, all we have, all the good we accomplish is given us, and we can never boast of it. "*What have you that you did not receive? If then you received it, why do you boast as if it were not a gift?*"[56]

A few months before her death, one of the sisters asked St. Thérèse of Lisieux what it means to be a small child before God. Thérèse mentioned several aspects of smallness, among them this:

> To be little is not attributing to oneself the virtues that one practices, believing oneself capable of anything, but to recognize that God places this treasure in the hands of His little child to be used when necessary; but it remains always God's treasure.[57]

We don't always think this way spontaneously. We tend to make ourselves the owners of God's gifts—for example, by using the good we accomplish to make a little pedestal for us to stand on, judging others and thinking ourselves superior to them! To rejoice in the good we do is legitimate, but not using it to feed our pride and disdain for others.

Notice the marvelous linkage in St. Thérèse's words between spiritual poverty and humility on the one hand

---

56. 1 Cor 4:7.

57. Thérèse of Lisieux, *Conversations*, August 6.8.

and gratitude on the other hand. When we are poor of heart, we are always grateful. We consider nothing as ours by right, since we know we are not worthy of anything, we lack all merit—and so we consider all the good in our lives as a gift, and this feeds our gratitude. Instead of attributing the good that we do to ourselves and glorying in it, we perceive it simply as an amazing gift from God, and we rejoice. This is Mary's attitude: "*He who is mighty has done great things for me*"![58]

So, too, nothing makes us grow more in humility than gratitude. Giving thanks to God involves attributing everything to him, recognizing that everything comes from his generous love. True humility has nothing to do with sadness. On the contrary, it is a source of joy, the joy of receiving everything freely from the hand of God and thanking him for it. As Father Raniero Cantalamessa says:

> [Praise] immolates and destroys man's pride! Whoever offers praise sacrifices to God the most acceptable victim that could exist and that is, his own glory. This is what the extraordinary purifying power of praise consists of. Humility is concealed in praise.[59]

---

58. Lk 1:49.
59. Raniero Cantalamessa, *Life in Christ: A Spiritual Commentary on the Letter to the Romans*, trans. Frances Lonergan Villa (Collegeville, Minn.: Liturgical Press, 2016), 7.5, EPUB.

This points to a question: Why are we so strongly inclined to use God's gifts to inflate our ego? For certain, this comes from the psychological need for recognition. Our lives and our individuality must have value in our own eyes and in the eyes of others. This is a legitimate need, but the customary way of satisfying it—seeking glory in our good works—is not the legitimate way and never succeeds.

My personal value is not derived from my efforts to bolster and nourish my ego, but from understanding that I am a child of God, freely loved and receiving all his mercy. The only real riches are God's infinite love for us and the words he addresses to us: "*All that is mine is yours*"![60] This is a treasure no one can take from us. It is a mistake to pretend that we have created this treasure ourselves and made ourselves rich by our own efforts. This way leads to failure. God and his inexhaustible mercy should alone be our true riches.

> Do not lay up for yourselves treasures on earth, where moth and rust consume and where thieves break in and steal, but lay up for yourselves treasures in heaven, where neither moth nor rust consumes and where

---

60. Lk 15:31.

thieves do not break in and steal. For where your treasure is, there will your heart be also.[61]

We save ourselves many worries and torments if we give up constantly looking in a mirror, asking ourselves if we are or aren't worthy, fretting about what others think of us, and instead look only to God and welcome him into our lives.

THE MORE WE ARE POOR, THE MORE WE ARE RICH

The more we are poor in ourselves, the more we become rich in the gifts of God. Often it is our lack of humility that prevents God from generously giving us all he would like. Moses' humility makes it possible for God to confide in him so much. Here is what Catherine de Bar says on the subject:

> God doesn't ask for anything better than to fill us with himself and his graces, but he sees us so full of pride and self-esteem that it stops him from communicating with us. For unless a soul is rooted in nothing but true humility and contempt for itself, it cannot receive God's gifts. Its self-love devours it,

61. Mt 6:19–21.

and God is obliged to leave it in its poverty, darkness, and sterility, keeping it in its nothingness, so necessary is a humble disposition.[62]

To be poor in spirit means accepting total dependence on God's mercy. It means having nothing, being nothing on one's own, but receiving everything, fully realizing the complete beneficence of God's gifts, which we could never deserve. Paradoxically, this is the source of freedom and happiness. We no longer need to worry about ourselves.

> We always want to be something. . . . Nothing in the world is rarer than to find a person content to be nothing by being entirely for God within. All is in God, and God depends on nothing. Here is all my worth, and my only joy is that, whatever happens, nothing should interrupt this, not even my imperfections and sins. Hope for nothing in yourself, but everything in Our Lord Jesus Christ.[63]

---

62. Mectilde de Bar, *Adorer et Adhérer,* p. 113.

63. Mectilde de Bar, p. 116.

Useless Servants

The parable of the "unworthy servant" in the Gospel of Luke sheds important light on poverty of spirit in our relationship with God.

> Will any one of you, who has a servant plowing or keeping sheep, say to him when he has come in from the field, "Come at once and sit down at table"? Will he not rather say to him, "Prepare supper for me, and gird yourself and serve me, till I eat and drink; and afterward you shall eat and drink"? Does he thank the servant because he did what was commanded? So you also, when you have done all that is commanded you, say, "We are unworthy servants; we have only done what was our duty."[64]

Probably this isn't a favorite among Jesus' parables since it doesn't seem fair to the poor servant who is so put upon. We would prefer that the master praise him warmly when he returns from work and let him get some rest. But be consoled: other Gospel passages take an approach very different from this parable. For instance: "*Blessed are those servants whom the master finds awake when he comes; truly, I say to you, he will*

---

64. Lk 17:7–10.

gird himself and have them sit at table, and he will come and serve them.[65] No need to doubt the goodness of the master toward servants who have done good work for him—they will receive even more than they deserve.

So what does this parable mean? Despite its apparent severity, it is, like all Jesus' parables, a narrative of love and freedom.

For one thing, it invites us not to think of ourselves as indispensable, which, in the end, is a very liberating thought. Considering ourselves indispensable gives rise to worries from which the Lord wants to deliver us.

But above all Jesus is telling us that the work we do for the good Lord (or for others) does not give us a right to anything—some particular consideration or reward. Doing good earns us recognition, but not a reward. The relationship with God is based freely giving and receiving, not on some trade or *quid pro quo*.

One who lacks this perspective is at risk of having a life of unhappiness and disappointment. The relationship with God will be founded on some kind of bookkeeping: two columns, one showing what we've given, the other what we've received. We shall never be satisfied with the balance, since the psychological wounds

---

65. Lk 12:37.

resulting from our comparisons—our jealousy, our self-love—won't allow it.

On the other hand, if I say to myself, "I've only done my duty, I am a useless servant, the good I've done is a pure gift of God who allowed me to do it and I have nothing that comes from myself," then I shall feel free and always satisfied. If, as Jesus says, my right hand does not know what my left hand is doing,[66] if I don't fret over comparing what I give and what I receive, if I have no rights arising from what I've given, I'll always be happy. I have received a lot, not because of some accumulation of merit on my part but by the generosity of God. We always come out ahead in attributing everything to God's generosity rather than our own merit! The one is infinite; the other very limited.

Here is an important aspect of poorness of heart: claiming nothing, demanding nothing in return for the good we have done. We do what we need to do, and for the rest we trust God entirely. And this isn't always easy to do, since it requires much detachment and much trust in God.

Someone poor in spirit accepts salvation as pure mercy, not as something given as a result of merit or

---

66. Mt 6:3.

personal good works. Such a person receives salvation as a grace, not as a right or the result of his or her efforts. This individual always stands before God with empty hands, knowing that the ability to serve God (rather than the world or the self), is in itself an unmerited grace, and that any recompense for service (and there will be one) is given altogether freely.

A poor person does not look upon his good deeds as props to bolster his self-esteem but instead looks to God's mercy as his sole support. Consider something Thérèse of Lisieux wrote during her last illness. Prevented by fatigue from fulfilling her duty to recite the office of the dead for her community's deceased, she found this a grace.

> I can depend on nothing, on no good works of my own in order to have confidence. For example, I'd like to be able to say that I've carried out all my obligations of reciting my prayers for the dead. This poverty, however, was a real light and a grace for me. I was thinking that never in my life would I be able to pay my debts to God; this was real riches, real strength for me, if I wanted to take it in this way. Then I made this prayer to God: O my God, I beg You, pay the debt that I have acquired with regard to the souls in purgatory, but do it as God, so that it be infinitely better than if I had said my Offices for the Dead. And then I remembered

with great consolation these words of St. John of the Cross' canticle: "Pay all debts." I had always applied this to Love. I felt this grace can't be expressed in words; it's far too sweet! We experience such great peace when we're totally poor, when we depend upon no one except God.[67]

This is not laziness, as the following from her Yellow Notebook makes clear:

Oh! How few perfect religious there are, who do nothing, or next to nothing, saying: I'm not obliged to do that, after all. There's no great harm in speaking here, in satisfying myself there. How few there are who do everything in the best way possible! And still these are the most happy religious.[68]

Here we see Thérèse's wonderful equilibrium: great generosity and fidelity even in little things, but a confidence that always rests only on God and not on her own works.

Always we are God's debtors, not with anguished guilt but in trust and filial joy, glad to be sustained by him and not by our own efforts. We are happy to

---

67. Thérèse of Lisieux, *Conversations*, August 6.4.
68. Thérèse of Lisieux, *Conversations*, August 6.5.

owe him everything, because we make no pretense of self-sufficiency and are like little children, content to receive everything from the generous hand of our father and to depend entirely on him for everything. Poverty is happiness because it makes us totally dependent on God and more completely attaches us to him. The goal of life is not to glorify ourselves or be satisfied with ourselves, but to glorify the infinite mercy of God to whom we owe everything.

To be Poor in Relation to One's Self

What does poverty in spirit in relation to one's self mean? As we have seen, it means putting aside self-regard and thinking only about God's free love for us: putting all our trust in God and not in ourselves.

It is essential that one recognize—and always accept—one's poorness and limitations, accepting myself as I am in my radical weakness, my fragility, and being reconciled to it, since I place my trust not in myself and my personal perfection but only in God.

Let's listen to Thérèse of Lisieux's words addressed to her sister Mary of the Sacred Heart, who was also her godmother. Thérèse had shared with her the burning desire for martyrdom that she felt during a retreat.

Ah! I really feel that it is not this at all that pleases God in my little soul; what pleases Him is *that He sees me loving my littleness* and my *poverty, the blind hope that I have in His mercy.* . . . That is my only treasure, dear Godmother, why would this treasure not be yours? . . .

We must consent to remain always poor and without strength, and this is the difficulty, for: "The truly poor in spirit, where do we find him? You must look for him from afar," said the psalmist. . . . He does not say that you must look for him among great souls, but "from afar," that is to say in *lowliness*, in *nothingness*. . . . Ah! let us remain then *very far* from all that sparkles, let us love our littleness, let us love to feel nothing, then we shall be poor in spirit, and Jesus will come to look for us, and *however far* we may be, He will transform us in flames of love. . . . Oh! how I would like to be able to make you understand what I feel! . . .[69]

Here is a beautiful expression of how being satisfied with littleness and grounded in total confidence in God attracts divine grace, which can transform us and lead us to summits of love that we would otherwise

---

69. Thérèse of Lisieux, *General Correspondence Volume Two*, LT 197.

be incapable of attaining by our own strength. Radical poverty, understood and accepted, is the font for an outpouring of the Holy Spirit.

In this way our poverty—not denied or fled from but lived, in expectation of God's mercy—becomes our salvation. Not a handicap but an opportunity! This is what allows St. Paul, declaring that God's power is "made perfect in weakness," to say: *I will all the more gladly boast of my weaknesses, that the power of Christ may rest upon me. . . . When I am weak, then I am strong.*[70]

This does not mean that we give up on improving ourselves or allow ourselves to sink into laziness or mediocrity. Yet we should never despair or become anxious at experiencing our human limitations. We must accept them and profit from them by placing all our hope in the Lord.

To Be Poor in Relation to One's Neighbor

Poverty of heart with regard to others is expressed in many ways. Here are a few, which we shall examine more deeply when we meditate on each of the Beatitudes.

---

70. 2 Cor 12:9–10.

One way, evoked by the sixth Beatitude, is to refuse to possess or appropriate the other—to renounce all manner of manipulating and using the other for our own ends.

The personhood of the other rules out our ever exploiting him or her to satisfy our own interests. Certainly we can accept from another what he or she can give us (and sometimes that is the immense gift of his or her own presence, affection, and support), but this gift must be freely given. Therefore, I must deny myself any use of the other for my own ends, subtle and subconscious as that may be, by pressuring the other person to give me what I want, instead of respecting his or her "otherness." (This can be seen in blackmail, seduction, reproach, sulking, etc.) It is fair to embrace what is given, but not to "take."

I must accept the fact that the other, no matter how close to me, is always beyond my reach and—happily!—never entirely fits the box I wish to impose on him or her. This kind of poverty is a grace because it requires me to be in a state of constant conversion and openness to the uniqueness of the other person, who cannot be reduced to a part of my personal universe, and obliges not to demand from the other to give me what only God can give me.

Poverty of heart consists of renouncing any hold over the other person and waiting for him or her, with meekness and patience, without compelling or appropriating the other. This person only belongs to me insofar as he or she freely gives himself or herself to me. I cannot impose anything. To be sure, there are situations in which, due to some duty we have to another (to provide for his or her education, to exercise legitimate authority in social or ecclesial life) we can demand or impose some things. But this is done in service to the common good and for the good of the person, and never for our own gratification. The service then is performed with respect and it is directed to him or her, not to oneself. "*For though I am free from all men, I have made myself a slave to all,*" St. Paul says.[71]

Being poor in regard to another also means humbling oneself lovingly. In the first chapter of *Story of a Soul* Thérèse of Lisieux says: "*the nature of love is to humble oneself.*"[72] Rather than seeking to domineer from a position of superiority, one must make oneself small before the other, in a spirit of humility and service. Like Jesus, washing the feet of his disciples, said: "*I*

---

71. 1 Cor 9:19.

72. Thérèse of Lisieux, *Story of a Soul*, loc. 740 of 6540.

am among you as one who serves."[73] And another time: "*He who is greatest among you shall be your servant.*"[74] St. Paul expressed the idea like this: "*Let no one seek his own good, but the good of his neighbor.*"[75]

In John's gospel, St. John the Baptist illustrates this attitude of poverty and detachment well, stepping aside to make way for Christ, joyfully accepting that the crowds, and even his own disciples, leave him to follow Jesus. He makes claims on no one but seeks to lead them to Christ.

> Now a discussion arose between John's disciples and a Jew over purifying. And they came to John, and said to him, "Rabbi, he who was with you beyond the Jordan, to whom you bore witness, here he is, baptizing, and all are going to him." John answered, "No one can receive anything except what is given him from heaven. You yourselves bear me witness, that I said, I am not the Christ, but I have been sent before him. He who has the bride is the bridegroom; the friend of the bridegroom, who stands and hears him, rejoices greatly at the bridegroom's voice; therefore this joy of mine is now full. He must increase, but I must decrease.[76]

---

73. Lk 22:27.
74. Mt 23:11.
75. 1 Cor 10:24.
76. Jn 3:25–30.

Mercy and forgiveness toward neighbors are essential aspects of poverty of heart. Renouncing resentment and the desire for vengeance while forgiving debts requires a large supply of it. (We shall return to this when speaking about the fifth Beatitude, concerning the merciful.)

Practicing poverty toward one's neighbor also means not having to have the last word all the time, setting aside the prideful insistence that one always be right. It means accepting being misunderstood, without always needing to justify ourselves. It means keeping silence. Yes, sometimes we must express ourselves in order to dispel misunderstandings and establish the truth of something the other person may not have perceived. But when we speak up, it should not be to show how clever we are or claim some supposed right of ours. We must know how to turn things over to God without always being understood and accepted by those around us.

We should love being hidden, known only by God, since often what is most beautiful and most precious is also most hidden. May our lives be hidden in God! "*But when you fast, anoint your head and wash your face, that your fasting may not be seen by men but by your Father who is in secret; and your Father who sees in secret will reward you.*"[77]

---

77. Mt 6:17–18.

Generosity is one of the most beautiful forms of poverty of heart. Recall the words of Jesus:

> "If any one would sue you and take your coat, let him have your cloak as well; and if any one forces you to go one mile, go with him two miles. Give to him who begs from you, and do not refuse him who would borrow from you."[78]

Of course, we cannot always give others what they want; often we allow ourselves to be imprisoned by human calculations, fears, and avarice. Being more free and generous carries with it a stronger experience of the faithfulness and providence of God.

POVERTY IN RELATION TO LIFE

Finally, let us turn to poverty of spirit in facing up to life and all that it brings—the joys and pains, what is happy and what is difficult. In the end, the poverty of which we speak is simply a right relationship with existence.

The right attitude toward the good things life brings is to embrace them with simplicity and thanksgiving, but not to cling to anything in a possessive

---

78. Mt 5:40–42.

or anxious manner. Job says: "*The Lord gave, and the Lord has taken away; blessed be the name of the Lord.*"[79] This is freedom in a spirit of detachment. The only good to which we must absolutely attach ourselves is God; all else is relative. Embrace what God gives, certainly, but in such a way that one's heart is not enslaved to anything.

To be poor requires that we accept the austerities that life can bring our way: material, emotional, spiritual, etc. Sometimes one may have to make a choice for poverty (as in taking religious vows, for those called to them), but the true poverties are not those we choose for ourselves, but those life imposes on us. These poverties, these losses, deceptions, or sufferings, even though difficult, are sources of grace when we accept them. From them we learn that the love and faithfulness of God are the only wealth that can fulfill our desires, enriching us as nothing and nobody else can do.

Think of Jesus' words to Peter:

Truly, truly, I say to you, when you were young, you girded yourself and walked where you would; but when you are old, you will stretch out your hands,

---

79. Jb 1:21.

and another will gird you and carry you where you
do not wish to go.[80]

In context, this is a prediction of the apostles'
deaths as martyrs, but it can also be understood in a
more general sense as Christ's invitation to follow him
on a life's journey that may lead us where we would
not otherwise have chosen to go.

Being poor means accepting the fact that we are
not the masters of our own lives and do not totally
control them. We in the West have an obsession with
control—planning everything, choosing everything,
and making all things subject to our wills. Yet this
is impossible, no matter how highly advanced we
become technologically. The pretension to being
all-powerful can lead only to disappointment and
anguish. Instead we need to wake up to the fact that
it's precisely the situations that we cannot control
that contribute most to our growth. Unable to change
what lies outside us, we must change ourselves. And in
the end this is what matters.

To be poor means knowing how to abandon oneself, trustingly allowing oneself to be led along the
unforeseen pathways of life, and saying yes to reality.

---

80. Jn 21:18.

Human wisdom gives way to the mysterious wisdom of God. When we cease playing at being life's masters and consent to embrace what comes to us day by day, life becomes full of meaning and beauty. "*Whoever seeks to gain his life will lose it, but whoever loses his life will preserve it.*"[81] This means coming to terms with not understanding everything and not having answers to all our questions. It means accepting a certain poverty of knowledge and abandoning ourselves in faith. This too finds expression as a beatitude: "*Blessed are those who have not seen and yet believe.*"[82]

Now and then ask yourself this question: What is my foundational attitude toward life? Many of us are like people at a reception who are offered a big tray with several dishes. Some we like a lot, others not so much. We are tempted to set aside what we don't like and take more of what we like.

You can do that with a platter of food, but you can't do it with life—and trying would result in a catastrophe. On what basis would we make our choices? Do we really know what's good for us? Everyone has had the experience of craving things that were big flops when

---

81. Lk 17:33.
82. Jn 20:29.

we actually obtained them, and trying to avoid things the proved to be precious opportunities for human and spiritual growth. The task isn't to filter out aspects of our lives but, as Thérèse of Lisieux put it, to "choose everything"—to welcome it all and not just put up with some things reluctantly. "*Accept whatever is brought upon you, and in changes that humble you be patient.*"[83]

The best, the most fruitful, exercise of freedom is not found in choosing but in consenting. And not passively or fatalistically either, but with trust in life as a gift from God. Of course one must sometimes choose to do good and avoid evil, and we must also do what we can to remedy negative situations in which we find ourselves (if you're sick, try to get well), but all this should be done in a spirit of acceptance, cultivating a good spirit and rejecting a bad one.

Another way of living poverty of spirit is to consent to the present moment, without trying to return to the past or plan the future. We possess only the present. We should accept the past and trust the future to divine providence. Don't stockpile provisions. Forget the way already traveled and set out afresh each day. Don't boast about the good

---

83. Sir 2:4.

accomplished or worry about the evil committed, but begin again each morning believing, hoping, and loving.

Finally, to be poor means not tying security to any particular thing. The more we seek human security, the more anxious we become. Our only security is the infinite mercy of God. We must of course embrace other things when they come—material goods, talents, qualities, virtues, skills, education, relationships, friendships, emotional support, institutions—and we must obtain these things when to do so is legitimate, but we must never base security on them or consider them to be some sort of bedrock we can trust. Our only definitive support is the mercy of God. Hear the words of St. John Eudes:

> Do not rely on the power or influence of friends, on your own money, on your intellect, knowledge or strength, on your good desires and resolutions, or on human means, or on any created thing, but on God's mercy alone. You may, of course, use all these things and take advantage of every aid that you can marshal on your side to conquer vice, to practice virtue, to direct and conclude all the business that God has placed in your hands, and acquit yourself of the obligations of your state in life. But you must renounce

all dependence or confidence you may have in these things, to rely upon Our Lord's goodness alone.[84]

POVERTY IN SPIRIT AND THEOLOGICAL VIRTUES

To conclude our reflection on spiritual poverty, let us look at it in relation to the theological virtues of faith, hope, and charity. They are the heart of the Christian life. They create in us all of God's riches, and yet a certain mystery of poverty attaches to their exercise.

Faith presupposes poverty of a certain kind. To believe means accepting that we don't always see and don't always understand, walking often in darkness. It means making progress by relying on another, handing oneself over to a truth that surpasses us which we don't totally understand. It means obedience of a sort, basing our lives on the words of others, dispossessing ourselves. Abraham, our father in the faith, set out not knowing his destination.

Hope is also a form of poverty. To hope means not to possess, but waiting in trust for what we don't yet possess, as Paul says in his letter to the Romans: "*For*

---

84. John Eudes, *The Life and Kingdom of Jesus in Christian Souls* (CreateSpace Independent Publishing, 2013), p. 57.

in this hope we were saved. Now hope that is seen is not hope. For who hopes for what he sees? But if we hope for what we do not see, we wait for it with patience."[85]

Love, too, presupposes a certain interior poverty. To love means to live not for oneself but for the other. Deciding to love someone means consenting to dependence, renouncing self-sufficiency. True love requires renunciation of all domination, all power over the other, all possessiveness, and obliges us to respect the freedom of the other.

If the theological virtues give rise to a certain form of poverty, poverty for its part is the fertile ground in which the theological virtues flourish. If poverty is a grace, it's because it requires us not to live as we are accustomed to do, not to content ourselves with the resources we find congenial, but to believe, hope, and love in a deeper and more pure way. It is the occasion for practicing the theological virtues in all their intensity and fruitfulness.

So meditating on poverty of spirit and the Beatitudes sheds light on how to practice faith, hope, and love in our daily lives. Let us continue our journey.

---

85. Rom 8:24–25.

2

HAPPY ARE THOSE WHO MOURN, FOR THEY WILL BE CONSOLED

Weeping may tarry for the night, but joy comes with the morning.[1]

Thou hast turned for me my mourning into dancing; thou hast loosed my sackcloth and girded me with gladness.[2]

Thy consolations cheer my soul.[3]

A Promise of Consolation

The second Beatitude is a promise of consolation for the afflicted. All tears, all afflictions will one day be

---

1. Ps 30:5.
2. Ps 30:11.
3. Ps 94:19.

the object of consolation originating with God himself. The fulfillment of this promise of consolation can sometimes take time to be realized. We must persevere in hope and patience. "*My eyes fail with watching for thy promise; I ask, 'When wilt thou comfort me?*"[4] God's time is not always our time. But God is faithful, and the moment of comfort will certainly come. "*May those who sow in tears reap with shouts of joy!*"[5]

The theme of consolation, in the Old Testament as in the New, is one of the most beautiful in Scripture.

It begins to appear chiefly in the second half of Isaiah, starting around chapter 40, in what might be called the "Book of Israel's Consolation." After the ruination of Jerusalem and the destruction of the temple, the tone of the prophetic text changes from vigorous invitations to conversion and threats of punishment to a message of consolation and hope once the hardship has arrived.

> Comfort, comfort my people, says your God. Speak tenderly to Jerusalem, and cry to her that her warfare is ended, that her iniquity is pardoned, that she has received from the LORD's hand double for all her sins.[6]

---

4. Ps 119:82.
5. Ps 126:5.
6. Is 40:1–2.

The rest of the passage invites us to "*prepare the way of the Lord*," to make ourselves available to God's future intervention on behalf of his people. He will come with force and tenderness, like a shepherd leading his flock:

> Behold, the Lord GOD comes with might, and his arm rules for him; behold, his reward is with him, and his recompense before him. He will feed his flock like a shepherd, he will gather the lambs in his arms, he will carry them in his bosom, and gently lead those that are with young.[7]

The theme comes up again several times later in the book:

> Sing for joy, O heavens, and exult, O earth; break forth, O mountains, into singing! For the LORD has comforted his people, and will have compassion on his afflicted. But Zion said, "The LORD has forsaken me, my Lord has forgotten me." Can a woman forget her sucking child, that she should have no compassion on the son of her womb? Even these may forget, yet I will not forget you.[8]

The most tender words expressing the mystery of God who consoles his weary children are in chapter 66.

---

7. Is 40:10–11.
8. Is 49:13–15.

This passage deeply touched Thérèse of Lisieux, and she cites it several times.

> Behold, I will extend prosperity to her like a river, and the wealth of the nations like an overflowing stream; and you shall suck, you shall be carried upon her hip, and dandled upon her knees. As one whom his mother comforts, so I will comfort you; you shall be comforted in Jerusalem.[9]

In the Jewish tradition, the Consoler (in Hebrew, Menahem מֶחֱנַמ) is one of the names for the Messiah. This Hebrew word has become a first name, still in use in the Jewish world today. The story of Jesus' presentation in the temple in Luke's gospel tells of an old man named Simeon, just and devout, who was "*looking for the consolation* of Israel." He had the good fortune to see the realization of his hope the day he held Jesus in his arms, in fulfillment of a promise by the Holy Spirit that he would not die before seeing Christ, the Lord's Messiah.[10]

St. Paul preaches often on the theme of divine consolation. He calls God the one "*who comforts the*

---

9. Is 66:12–13.
10. Lk 2:25–26.

downcast,"[11] "*the God of steadfastness and encourage-ment,*"[12] and asks God's consolation for the Christians of Thessalonica in these words:

> Now may our Lord Jesus Christ himself, and God our Father, who loved us and gave us eternal comfort and good hope through grace, comfort your hearts and establish them in every good work and word.[13]

This consolation is understood as a renewal of hope, of which the Scriptures are one of the principal sources: "*For whatever was written in former days was written for our instruction, that by steadfastness and by the encour-agement of the scriptures we might have hope.*"[14]

Later we shall consider Paul's principal passage on this subject, the first chapter of the Second Letter to the Corinthians.

The concluding chapters of the book of Revelation (principally a message of consolation and hope for a persecuted Church) adopts from Isaiah a description of God as he who "*wipe[s] away tears from all faces,*"[15]

---

11. 2 Cor 7:6.

12. Rom 15:5.

13. 2 Thes 2:16–17.

14. Rom 15:4.

15. Is 25:8.

and contain a magnificent passage on the consolation God will give at the coming of his Kingdom and the New Jerusalem:

> Then I saw a new heaven and a new earth; for the first heaven and the first earth had passed away, and the sea was no more. And I saw the holy city, new Jerusalem, coming down out of heaven from God, prepared as a bride adorned for her husband; and I heard a great voice from the throne saying, "Behold, the dwelling of God is with men. He will dwell with them, and they shall be his people, and God himself will be with them; he will wipe away every tear from their eyes, and death shall be no more, neither shall there be mourning nor crying nor pain any more, for the former things have passed away." And he who sat upon the throne said, "Behold, I make all things new."[16]

THE SUFFERING AND CONSOLING MESSIAH

It is noteworthy that in the book of Isaiah the theme of consolation in the second part of the book (starting

---

16. Rv 21:1–5.

with chapter 40, which begins with the words: *Comfort, comfort my people*) coincides with the emergence of another very important theme: the "suffering savior," a mysterious, elect person coming from God, anointed by the Holy Spirit to free captives and be light for the nations, who nevertheless undergoes humiliation and suffering: "*He was despised and rejected by men; a man of sorrows, and acquainted with grief. . . . He was oppressed, and he was afflicted, yet he opened not his mouth; like a lamb that is led to the slaughter.*"[17] This passage represents the community of Israel but also prefigures the suffering Messiah who is fulfilled in the person of Christ. Having taken upon himself our suffering, he bears a grace of consolation and peace:

> The Lord GOD has given me the tongue of those who are taught, that I may know how to sustain with a word him that is weary.[18]

> Upon him was the chastisement that made us whole, and with his stripes we are healed.[19]

---

17. Is 53:3–7.
18. Is 50:4.
19. Is 53:5.

The simultaneous presence of these two themes in the second part of Isaiah reveals something fundamental: the source of all true consolation is found in the mystery of the Lord's Passion. Because of his suffering on the cross, there is no longer any human pain or suffering that cannot be consoled, provided we trustingly approach Jesus or allow ourselves to be visited by him. Someone who suffers a trial will ultimately experience the consolation and reassurance he or she needs in Jesus. As the Letter to the Hebrews says: "*Because he himself has suffered and been tempted, he is able to help those who are tempted.*"[20] And again: "*For we have not a high priest who is unable to sympathize with our weaknesses, but one who in every respect has been tempted as we are, yet without sinning.*"[21]

This appears to suggest that divine consolation does not come only to put an end to suffering, as if suffering and consolation were two opposed things foreign to each other. Rather, it is something born out of suffering, provided suffering is accepted in faith and lived in communion with the Lord. The cross is a cruel and brutal reality, but out of it flow rivers of

20. Heb 2:18.
21. Heb 4:15.

consolation and peace on those who contemplate it with faith, recognizing in it the indisputable sign of God's love and faithfulness.

What Are the Tears that Receive Consolation?

The second Beatitude points to a question. What shedding of tears is Jesus talking about? What is this weeping that will be the object of divine consolation?

Several responses are possible.

First, there are the tears of repentance. When the human heart is touched by the grace of repentance, when it realizes the gravity of its sin, when it recognizes its pride, its hardness, its egotism, and begins to lament sincerely over its faults, it receives the grace of consolation and peace very quickly.

True repentance moves me to throw myself at the feet of the Lord and invoke his mercy. This is when I experience his speedy pardon and tenderness: and my tears of repentance purify and free my heart. The sinful woman of the Gospel who threw herself at the feet of Jesus, washed them in her tears, bathed them in perfume and dried them with her hair, received immense consolation when the Lord told her "*Your sins are forgiven. . . . Your faith has saved you, go in peace.*"[22]

"*He who cries over his sins is greater than he who revives the dead,*" the Desert Fathers said. They compared such tears to a new baptism in which the heart was washed of its faults. "*They wash the heart, purify the body, heal the sick soul.*"[23]

Tears obtain the consolation of experiencing the Lord's infinite mercy, his fatherly tenderness that welcomes back the prodigal son, of feeling washed and purified, reconciled with oneself, and finding that, even if "*our hearts condemn us . . . God is greater than our hearts.*"[24] The mercy of God will always be greater than my sin; "*where sin increased, grace abounded all the more.*"[25]

To weep over one's sin is a great grace. Of course we can't measure repentance only by physical criteria; repentance lies in honest recognition of our faults and a will to correct them. That said, however, when the tears we shed are real, as were St. Peter's after his

---

22. Lk 7:48–50.

23. Matta el-Maskîne, *L'expérience de Dieu dans la vie de prière* (Bégrolles-en-Mauges, France: Abbaye de Bellefontaine, 1996).

24. 1 Jn 3:20.

25. Rom 5:20.

denials, this is an immense benefit. We should ask for this grace that makes our hardness of heart melt away.

Tears of compassion are another form of consoling tears. "*Weep with those who weep*," St. Paul says.[26] To be moved and touched by the suffering of another, in such a way that we are actually driven to take care of him or her, this too brings the grace of consolation. When compassion is not merely a feeling but becomes efficacious love that reaches out to the other, the joy of freely loving is born within us. "*It is more blessed to give than to receive*," St. Paul says, repeating what the Lord said.[27] And Jesus tells us: "*When you give a feast, invite the poor, the maimed, the lame, the blind, and you will be blessed, because they cannot repay you.*"[28] It is often in consoling others that we ourselves are consoled.

Sometimes, when the tears come from love and the person's heart is touched by God's tenderness to the point of weeping, tears themselves are already a consolation. One of St. Thérèse of Lisieux's sisters found her one day deeply lost in thought. "*When I inquired, 'What are you thinking about?' she replied with tears in*

---

26. Rom 12:15.
27. Act 20:35.
28. Lk 14:13–14.

her eyes: 'I am meditating on the Our Father. It is so sweet to call God our Father!'[29]

In the Eastern churches the gift of tears is considered one of the most precious charisms and a sign of the Holy Spirit's presence. St. Arsenius, a former Roman senator who became a monk in Egypt in the fifth century, lost his eyelashes and his eyelids became withered from crying so much; he never ceased praying by shedding tears, as much in sweet, silent praise as in intercession for the suffering of all the world. The saints do not weep for themselves but for the suffering of humankind and because God is not sufficiently loved. "*My eyes shed streams of tears, because men do not keep thy law.*"[30] These tears are already a kind of consolation, for they are the expression of a very pure love.

THE FATHER OF MERCY AND GOD OF ALL CONSOLATION

Let's return now to the idea of consolation in relation to those tears that accompany affliction and suffering in which we began. We shall focus on St. Paul's

---

29. Thérèse of Lisieux and Sister Geneviève, *Conseils et souvenirs* (Paris: Les Éditions du Cerf, 2005), p. 81.

30. Ps 119:136.

most important passage about God as consoler of the afflicted, the first chapter of the Second Letter to the Corinthians. It deserves to be read carefully.

After the salutation, the text is a thanksgiving hymn, in the style typical of Jewish prayers of blessing, in which Paul thanks God for consoling him after a time of trial. Here he gives God one of the most beautiful titles in all of Scripture— *"Father of Mercies and God of all comfort."*[31]

> Blessed be the God and Father of our Lord Jesus Christ, the Father of mercies and God of all comfort, who comforts us in all our affliction, so that we may be able to comfort those who are in any affliction, with the comfort with which we ourselves are comforted by God.[32]

Verse 8 suggests the reason why Paul praises the Lord so highly—his deliverance from a very painful trial that he experienced in the Roman province of Asia, in the west of today's Turkey.

> For we do not want you to be ignorant, brethren, of the affliction we experienced in Asia; for we were so

---

31. 2 Cor 1:3.
32. 2 Cor 1:3–4.

utterly, unbearably crushed that we despaired of life itself. Why, we felt that we had received the sentence of death.[33]

Surprisingly, Paul gives no specifics regarding this extreme trial but tells us only that it was beyond his strength to bear (which says a lot, considering that it's Paul who says it) and could have cost his life. Illness? Mistreatment or stoning? Falling into the hands of a court with the power to inflict capital punishment? We don't know. A journalist today would make much of it, but Paul is not the kind of person to seek pity by making a tragedy of his life and presenting himself as a victim as is the fashion today. He mentions this trial only to encourage the believers with whom he is concerned by testifying to God's fidelity and to the good that can come from trials.

The first beneficial aspect of this suffering cited by the Apostle lies in having taught him to "*rely not on ourselves but on God who raises the dead.*"[34] Trials make us aware of our limitations, and invite us to lean only on God, and not on ourselves.

The next sentence—"*He delivered us from so deadly a peril, and he will deliver us; on him we have set our*

---

33. 2 Cor 1:8–9.
34. 2 Cor 1:9.

hope that he will deliver us again"[35]—points to another fruit of this trial for Paul. Having experienced the faithfulness of God who delivered him, he is strengthened in his hope for the future.

The passage concludes with verse 11: "*You also must help us by prayer, so that many will give thanks on our behalf for the blessing granted us in answer to many prayers.*" Aware that his deliverance from trial was no doubt due to the Christian community's prayers, he invites these people to give thanks. He has been shown how much we need prayer from others in difficult times; and his communion in prayer with these believers has been strengthened by his experience of tribulation and deliverance.

Paul's thanksgiving also speaks of other fruits from his trial:

> Blessed be the God and Father of our Lord Jesus Christ, the Father of mercies and God of all comfort, who comforts us in all our affliction, so that we may be able to comfort those who are in any affliction, with the comfort with which we ourselves are comforted by God. For as we share abundantly in Christ's sufferings, so through Christ we share abundantly in

---

35. 2 Cor 1:10.

comfort too. If we are afflicted, it is for your comfort
and salvation; and if we are comforted, it is for your
comfort, which you experience when you patiently
endure the same sufferings that we suffer.[36]

Delivered and consoled by God, Paul discovers that
this divine consolation empowers him to console others in their trials. Here is a beautiful fruit of the communion and charity born of his experience. All he went
through, whether trial or consolation, is not only for
him but for the others. This is very important: experiencing difficulty equips us to understand and comfort
others in their difficulties. The grace of compassion
and empathy is born of tribulations.

In sometimes permitting us to go through painful
trials, God intends that we not only realize our limitations and poverty but, even more, come to understand
others better, not judging them from afar but coming
near to those in difficulty.

Suffering involves isolation by placing us outside of
"normal" life. Those around us seem well and happy,
while I am alone with my distress. The greatest comfort
then is for someone to say to me, "I know what you're
going through, I get it. I've been there myself."

---

36. 2 Cor 1:3–6.

The point is not that one must have gone through every kind of suffering in order to understand others' suffering. But it is necessary that one have at least some suffering to grasp what it's like to find oneself down, alone, miserable, powerless, and destitute. Then one can approach others speaking the language of genuine understanding, not as false consolers, like Job's friends, who came to moralize and make his burden even heavier on the pretext of counseling him. Then one can have the right attitude, keeping still when we should and finding the right words when words are possible. Having the right attitude when faced with someone who is suffering is not easy. We may be fearful in the face of suffering or clumsy, hurting others more by what we say. To experience a painful trial and God's faithfulness, as St. Paul did, teaches a precious lesson in understanding others and effectively helping them.

Now a word about verse 7: "*Our hope for you is unshaken; for we know that as you share in our sufferings, you will also share in our comfort.*" What Paul lived through evidently strengthened him in his hope that if others who are dear to him go through suffering, they too will experience consolation.

Sometimes, faced with another's suffering, we are indifferent or passive. Our fear or our egotism may prevent us from responding. We distance ourselves and go on our way, like the priest and the Levite in the parable of the Good Samaritan, who passed by a man whom thieves had attacked and left half-dead by the side of the road.[37] Or sometimes perhaps we go to the other extreme and, too compassionate, we despair in the face of someone who is close to us.

In Paul we see the right attitude toward those for whom he cares. On the one hand, he is full of tenderness and compassion, as we often see in his letters:

> Who is weak, and I am not weak? Who is made to fall, and I am not indignant?[38]

> We were gentle among you, like a nurse taking care of her children. So, being affectionately desirous of you, we were ready to share with you not only the gospel of God but also our own selves, because you had become very dear to us.[39]

> My little children, with whom I am again in travail until Christ be formed in you![40]

---

37. Lk 10:30–31.
38. 2 Cor 11:29.
39. 1 Thes 2:7–8.
40. Gal 4:19.

On the other hand, Paul accepts the fact that his children are suffering and is never discouraged or worried because of it. He retains the same hopeful outlook on the suffering of others that he has toward his own suffering. God is faithful, and after the trying times will come the times of comfort and fruitfulness.

LOOKING FOR CONSOLATION IN GOD

Sometimes we do not receive divine consolation because we are too focused on getting it from other people. Scripture often makes the point that God alone is the true refuge and comfort of those in need—"*a stronghold to the poor, a stronghold to the needy in his distress.*"[41]

I'm not saying we should reject human help. True humility includes knowing that we all need the help of others. We should embrace the support and comfort given by those close to us, letting ourselves be consoled and loved with simplicity and humility. But we should not avidly seek it or, still worse, reproach others for not understanding us or helping us as we would like. God sometimes allows it that we not find support from others in order that we find our comfort solely in him.

---

41. Is 25:4.

Sometimes, too, we must be quiet during the trial, persevere in prayer, seek light and respite in the words of Scripture, and contemplate Christ's cross to find the way of consolation little by little. Instead of unburdening ourselves to others, we should sometimes shed our tears with God, as the psalm says: "*Thou hast kept count of my tossings; put thou my tears in thy bottle!*"[42]

God can give the gift of consolation through people whom we encounter along our way, but he may instead do this entirely by himself. Consolation is truly a work that belongs to the Holy Spirit. It is not just a matter of feelings but something more profound: it involves regaining peace, strength, and hope. Peace with what we have suffered in the past, strength for today, and hope for the future. To be consoled means realizing that our experience, bad as it seems, is really a precious good. It means giving thanks.

BECOME CONSOLERS

Finally, in concluding this reflection on the second Beatitude, let us consider the Christian vocation as a ministry of consolation. The consolation we receive

---

42. Ps 56:8.

from God is not for us to keep for ourselves. Rather, we in our turn are to become consolers of those who need it.

There is a great need for consolation in today's world. So much suffering, often hidden or denied, fails to find the consolation it needs. The cry of Scripture—"*I looked for pity, but there was none; and for comforters, but I found none*"[43]—is more timely now than ever. Most people stand more in need of consolation and encouragement than reproach. Certainly we must witness to the truth of the Gospel and keep in mind some necessary truths. But to be Christian doesn't mean forever lecturing others. It means reaching out in love and mercy to the world's distress and giving it confidence and hope.

If we fully live the Beatitudes, we will be in a position to become consolers of the broken-hearted. This is a beautiful part of the Christian vocation. The Church has a universal ministry of consolation. It is charged with proclaiming to all humankind the comforting words of Revelation: "*Weep not; lo, the Lion of the tribe of Judah, the Root of David, has conquered.*"[44]

---

43. Ps 69:20.
44. Rv 5:5.

The magnificent Messianic anointing described in the sixty-first chapter of Isaiah rests on Christ, on the Church, and on every baptized person, especially priests by virtue of their priesthood. It is more urgent than ever that it be spread abroad, but to do that we need poverty of heart.

> The Spirit of the Lord GOD is upon me,
> because the LORD has anointed me
> to bring good tidings to the afflicted;
> he has sent me to bind up the brokenhearted,
> to proclaim liberty to the captives,
> and the opening of the prison to those who are
>   bound;
> to proclaim the year of the LORD's favor,
> and the day of vengeance of our God;
> to comfort all who mourn;
> to grant to those who mourn in Zion—
> to give them a garland instead of ashes,
> the oil of gladness instead of mourning,
> the mantle of praise instead of a faint spirit.[45]

---

45. Is 61:1–3.

3

HAPPY ARE THE MEEK

One thing have I asked of the LORD,
that will I seek after;
that I may dwell in the house of the LORD
all the days of my life,
to behold the beauty of the LORD.[1]

Let the favor of the Lord our God be upon us.[2]

We have already spoken of meekness in speaking of Moses, the most humble and meek man in the world, and the Hebrew term *anava* which means poor, humble, or meek. Although it is one of the most precious expressions of love, it is unfortunately quite rare in today's hard, competitive world. Yet it remains a powerful tool for attracting and opening hearts.

---

1. Ps 27:4.
2. Ps 90:17.

God, Source of all Meekness

Meekness is above all a divine quality. In God there is "*consuming fire*"[3] that is also infinite meekness. The Psalms sometimes speak of it: "*Praise the Lord, for the Lord is good; sing to his name, for he is gracious!*"[4] And: "*Great is thy mercy, O Lord.*"[5] Scripture invites us to experience it: "*O taste and see that the Lord is good!*"[6]

God has a tenderness, a sensitivity surpassing anything we could imagine but experienced by saints and mystics. St. John of the Cross speaks in the *Living Flame*[7] of the extreme tenderness of the touch of the Word of God:

> O sweet cautery,
> O delightful wound!
> O gentle hand! O delicate touch
> that tastes of eternal life
> and pays every debt!

Meekness is also the characteristic attribute of the Holy Spirit's action. The Spirit is both forceful and

---

3. Heb 12:29.

4. Ps 135:3.

5. Ps 119:156.

6. Ps 34:8.

7. John of the Cross, "The Living Flame of Love," in *The Collected Works of St. John of the Cross*, trans. Kieran Kavanaugh, OCD, and Otilio Rodriguez, OCD (Washington, D.C.: ICS, 1991). Kindle.

meek. Paul includes it among his famous list of the fruits of the Spirit in the letter to the Galatians.[8]

The heart of Jesus is suffused with it. He speaks of meekness, associated with humility, as the principal quality of his soul in a beautiful passage:

> Come to me, all who labor and are heavy laden, and I will give you rest. Take my yoke upon you, and learn from me; for I am gentle and lowly in heart, and you will find rest for your souls. For my yoke is easy, and my burden is light.[9]

Crowds gathered around Jesus not only because of the healings he performed but also because of his meekness, which touched and opened hearts. Among some of the Pharisees and doctors of the law, and especially among the Sadducees, there was much arrogance and hardness toward the poor and sinners along with a great contempt for uneducated people, but with Jesus it was just the opposite: he welcomed these people with a welcome full of goodness. We sometimes see them delighted when Jesus silences the know-it-alls; here was payback for the harsh judgment and disdain these clever ones had heaped on them. The New Testament often refers

---

8. Gal 5:23.
9. Mt 11:28–30.

to Christ's meekness. Especially Paul: "*I, Paul, myself entreat you, by the meekness and gentleness of Christ.*"[10]

And this quality has its supreme expression in Christ's Passion. Jesus allows himself to be led to the sacrifice like a lamb who does not open his mouth—he who, "*when he was reviled . . . did not revile in return; when he suffered . . . did not threaten; but . . . trusted to him who judges justly.*"[11]

The Christian is invited to imitate Christ's meekness, so often associated with humility and patience: "*Put on then, as God's chosen ones, holy and beloved, compassion, kindness, lowliness, meekness, and patience*";[12] "*with all lowliness and meekness, with patience, forbearing one another in love.*"[13]

This meekness is especially asked of leaders of the Church,[14] who have the immense responsibility of being likenesses of Christ the good shepherd. Nothing is more opposed to pastoral charity, which the leaders of the Church must exhibit, than hardness, intransigence, or anger.

----

10. 2 Cor 10:1.

11. 1 Pt 2:23.

12. Col 3:12.

13. Eph 4:2.

14. 2 Tm 2:24–25.

Meekness can be practiced only by letting ourselves be filled with it by God. Contact with God, in prayer in particular, enables people little by little to discover the infinite meekness of God and themselves be clothed in this meekness, which progressively eliminates all manner of hardness and bitterness of heart. Only intimate contact with the heart of Jesus can heal the hardness of the human heart. Here is that "*[putting] on the Lord Jesus Christ*" of which Paul's wonderful expression speaks.[15]

"*A soul that is hard because of its self-love grows harder. O good Jesus, if you do not soften it, it will ever continue in its natural hardness*,"[16] St. John of the Cross said. The human heart can only be truly meek by letting itself be calmed by God, freed from agitation, fear, and worry. Humility, meekness, and peace are fruits of the Spirit that go together. Only the poor and humble heart can embrace divine peace and be a peacemaker for others.

We shall return to this when speaking of the seventh Beatitude: "*Blessed are the peacemakers, for they shall be called sons of God.*"[17]

The meekness of which the Gospel speaks is not wimpishness or weakness or cowardice. On the

---

15. Rom 13:14.

16. John of the Cross, Maxim p. 979. "The Sayings of Light and Love," nos. 30–31, in *Collected Works*.

17. Mt 5:9.

contrary, it requires great interior strength to resist anger and passion, to refrain from violent reactions. Not allowing oneself to be contaminated by violence requires great courage. Joan of Arc knew how to take up arms to deliver her country because that was necessary, but her heart was never touched by hate; she cared for the wounded English with love.

The Third Beatitude and Psalm 36

The third Beatitude is in fact a quotation from Psalm 37. Examining this psalm helps us understand it.

> Be still before the LORD, and wait patiently for him; fret not yourself over him who prospers in his way, over the man who carries out evil devices! Refrain from anger, and forsake wrath! Fret not yourself; it tends only to evil. For the wicked shall be cut off; but those who wait for the LORD shall possess the land. Yet a little while, and the wicked will be no more; though you look well at his place, he will not be there. But the meek shall possess the land, and delight themselves in abundant prosperity.[18]

---

18. Ps. 37:7–11.

This psalm raises a perennial question that is often found in the Old Testament: Why is there so much injustice in the world? Why do evildoers so often prosper while the just suffer?

The psalm invites those who encounter such situations not to be eaten up by anger and bitterness, which are only hurtful to themselves. The triumph of evil is only temporary. Remain calm and confident, place all your hope in the Lord. Evil will disappear, the meek will inherit the earth and will delight in great peace. Later in the psalm we again find the promise that the just will "possess the earth" (verse 29) as will those who hope in the Lord (verse 34).

We can sum up the psalm's invitation like this: however bad the situation you encounter may be, don't become agitated and angry, for that will just make things worse. Continue to be humble and meek, calm and peaceable, persevere in doing good and place your hope in God. In this way you will triumph. The earth will be given to you in return. Not that we haven't the right and duty to react strongly against injustice, but should do so without letting our hearts be invaded by bad feelings—irritation, resentment, loss of hope, etc.—that can ultimately make us too unjust, make us accomplices of that which we would resist.

THE MEEKNESS OF THE GOSPEL
AND ITS ATTRIBUTES

We can distinguish various aspects of meekness by looking at its opposites.

Meekness considered as the opposite of hardness is kindness, tenderness, benevolence. It is close to the beatitude of the merciful.

Meekness is also the opposite of bitterness, remaining peaceful and confident, rather than being consumed by rancor when faced with injustice or painful situations. In this way it is similar to the beatitude of the pure of heart and of the peacemakers.

Meekness is also the opposite of rigidness. It is the flexibility of the person who embraces things as they are, not reacting against the reality of things and events. People like this let themselves be guided. They are not stiff-necked but are open to being taught and guided, as the psalm says: "*He leads the humble in what is right, and teaches the humble his way.*"[19] Meekness in this way is related to poorness of spirit.

---

19. Ps 25:9.

What does "Possess the Earth" Mean?

The reward associated with the third Beatitude can be understood in several ways.

In one sense, it promises entry into the Promised Land, the Kingdom of Heaven. This promise is attached also to the first and eighth Beatitudes. Indeed, all the Beatitudes offer entry to God's Kingdom, the "land of milk and honey," a land of abundance where all God's promises will be fully realized and all our desires will be satisfied. For this kingdom is Christ himself, true "land of the living," according to the expression of the Orthodox theologian Olivier Clément.

The use of "land" to describe the kingdom recalls the Promised Land, so often described as a land of rest, where we shall find repose and peace after the struggle of our long exodus.

> The LORD gives rest to your brethren, as to you, and they also occupy the land which the LORD your God gives them beyond the Jordan; then you shall return every man to his possession which I have given you.[20]

A second way of understanding "will possess the earth" (or "will inherit the earth"—which is a reminder

---

20. Dt 3:20.

that to possess in this case is not a right but a free gift from God) is that meekness is a conqueror of hearts. Humility and meekness are capable of taming hearts repelled by hardness and pride. In Dostoyevsky's *The Brothers Karamazov* the wise monk Father Zōsima says:

> At some thoughts one stands perplexed, especially at the sight of men's sin, and wonders whether one should use force or humble love. Always decide to use humble love. If you resolve on that once for all, you may subdue the whole world. Loving humility is marvelously strong, the strongest of all things, and there is nothing else like it.[21]

A third way of interpreting possession of the earth is that for someone who lives the Beatitudes—a man of humble heart, poor and meek—all is well in the end. Every circumstance, fortunate or unfortunate, every success and failure, adds its bit to making him grow. Practicing the Beatitudes is the way to immense freedom. The poor person becomes a sovereign and tastes the sovereign liberty of the children of God.

St. Faustina expresses it like this:

---

21. Fyodor Dostoyevsky, *The Brothers Karamazov,* trans. Constance Garnett (Mineola, N.Y.: Dover, 2005), pp. 291–93.

Everything that exists on earth is at my service: friends, enemies, success, adversity . . . all things, willing or not, must serve me. I do not think of them at all; I strive to be faithful to God and to love Him to the point of complete forgetfulness of self. And He Himself looks after me and fights against my enemies.[22]

St. Paul already expresses this wonderful truth:

For all things are yours, whether Paul or Apol'los or Cephas or the world or life or death or the present or the future, all are yours; and you are Christ's and Christ is God's.[23]

And St. John of the Cross speaks of the "Christian kingship" that Baptism confers.

Mine are the heavens and mine is the earth. Mine are the nations, the just are mine, and mine the sinners. The angels are mine, and the Mother of God, and all things are mine; and God Himself is mine and for me, because Christ is mine and all for me. What do you ask, then, and seek, my soul? Yours is all of

---

22. Maria Faustina Kowalska, *Diary of Saint Maria Faustina Kowalska: Divine Mercy in My Soul* (Stockbridge, Mass.: Marian Press, 2014), no. 1720. Kindle.
23. 1 Cor 3:21–23.

this, and all is for you. Do not engage yourself in something less, nor pay heed to the crumbs that fall from your Father's table. Go forth and exult in your Glory! Hide yourself in it and rejoice, and you will obtain the supplications of your heart.[24]

MEEKNESS OPPOSED TO VENGEANCE

After the Beatitudes, Jesus extends a paradoxical invitation in the Sermon on the Mount. Although difficult to interpret, it gives a practical example of meekness:

You have heard that it was said, "An eye for an eye and a tooth for a tooth." But I say to you, Do not resist one who is evil. But if any one strikes you on the right cheek, turn to him the other also; and if any one would sue you and take your coat, let him have your cloak as well; and if any one forces you to go one mile, go with him two miles. Give to him who begs from you, and do not refuse him who would borrow from you.[25]

How are we to understand these words, which seem so unrealistic in a world where we must so often do battle?

24. John of the Cross, "The Sayings of Light and Love," no. 27, in *The Collected Works*.

25. Mt 5:38–42.

On a superficial level, the meaning is clear enough, though by no means easy to practice: we must not respond to evil with evil. Revenge causes evils to multiply and spread, while we become their accomplices. Only forgiveness halts the cycle of evil. (We shall return to this when discussing the Beatitude of the merciful.)

It seems, however, that Jesus has something more in mind.

It is not that he asks us to practice literally what he says (turn the other cheek, don't claim one's rights, and so on). It is sometimes legitimate to defend ourselves, and especially to defend the weak, against aggression and violence. It is sometimes necessary to claim one's rights, for example, taking legal action against an employer who doesn't pay me what I've earned.

But also in other situations the Holy Spirit invites us not to defend ourselves, not to protect ourselves, not to make any claims, to give more than what simple justice requires, in order to give oneself entirely to God.

But why is this sometimes necessary?

First of all, because to escape entrapment in our fears and defense mechanisms, in our avarice and our calculations, we must sometimes put these things aside for the sake of being truly free.

Furthermore, the Holy Spirit sometimes calls upon us to transcend the logic of fairness and simple justice and rise to a level of interior spiritual combat at which we fight ourselves instead of fighting others. In this way evil is defeated at its root and not simply in its manifestations—defeated by submitting to it as Jesus did in the knowledge that it is better to submit to evil than to commit it, and abundant love is the correct response to abundant evil.

Sometimes we shall have to accept certain injustices lest we become unjust in always demanding that we be given what we consider our due. This is not a general rule for every situation, but a particular call in some circumstances—yet a call that every disciple of Jesus must heed at certain points in his or her life.

Human justice cannot resolve all the world's problems. Only the madness of charity will get to the bottom of evil.

Sometimes we must simply insist on justice, for the love of Christ and our neighbor, for our own conversion, for love of peace. This may mean accepting it when we're misunderstood, judged or hurt, silently giving ourselves over to God who alone judges with justice. Thus we are freed from our calculations and our human defenses so that we enter into the poverty that empowers us to place ourselves entirely in God's hands.

At such times we are called to suffer injustice as a way of being in communion with Christ in his Passion.

Only an excess of love can save the world. And here we are already in the territory of the Beatitude of those who accept persecution. (But let us return to that later.)

MEEKNESS AND ANGER

One can hardly speak of meekness without saying a word about anger, since controlling anger is essential to the practice of meekness. Jesus puts it bluntly: "*You have heard that it was said to the men of old, 'You shall not kill; and whoever kills shall be liable to judgment.' But I say to you that every one who is angry with his brother shall be liable to judgment.*"[26]

To feel anger is normal—indeed, it's one of the most common emotions. But we cannot simply give into it, since anger can become sin (one of the seven capital sins that lead to many others). In doing so, it becomes destructive, for others and ourselves.

Yes, there is such a thing as holy anger. The gospels sometimes show Jesus as angry. But this is never on his own behalf but on behalf of little ones or fundamental

---

26. Mt 5:21–22.

spiritual realities such as the holiness of the Temple. God's anger is always directed against what is bad for us. He is not angry for himself but to protect people against themselves. But let's not imagine our own anger is always "holy anger." Often we become angry under the pretext of defending something essential when we are only acting out of self-love or to protect our interests.

At its most basic level, anger is the reaction of the animal defending his territory because it is necessary to his survival. It is also the normal reaction to injustice, expressing the need for justice and truth essential to life. But anger can become negative, lashing out violently at the other or masking an egotistical interest. When consumed by anger, we can do much harm to others and ourselves. An angry heart loses its peace, lucidity and freedom, and brings its progress in love to a halt.

Losing one's temper may be excusable, as St. Paul says, but the sun must not go down on our anger. "*Be angry but do not sin; do not let the sun go down on your anger, and give no opportunity to the devil.*"[27] Sometimes one can't help throwing a tantrum, but it's absolutely required that one go to sleep in peace. There is a duty to react against injustices, but a larger duty to

---

27. Eph 4:26–27.

maintain interior peace. This is the subject of the seventh Beatitude.

How do we manage our angry reactions? First we need to take note of our anger, know how to express it to ourselves, identify its causes, and sometimes speak with someone who can help us manage it. Anger that is unadmitted, unexpressed, and suppressed is destructive.

Then we need to ask ourselves this question: Just what good am I trying to defend with this anger? Is it a real, objective good or only something I've turned into a good to be defended at all costs when it's really nothing of the kind? Some people get angry at the breaking of any little rule of their particular group, but under pretext of defending the rule, they are defending their psychological need for security, as if, were the rule not respected, the whole world would collapse. (Rules are useful, but it's God's mercy, not rules, that saves the world.) The good defended by our anger is often nothing vital and sometimes illusory, in which case it's hardly worth making a fuss about.

If the good our anger is defending is objective and real, we need to ask a second question: Is it my responsibility to defend it? Sometimes we vex ourselves over causes whose defense isn't up to us, but someone else. It isn't my duty to save the whole world. Discerning what is and isn't our responsibility can be hard, but necessary.

Some things we need to stop worrying about and leave to someone else, or to God.

But if I'm angry in defense of a real good for which I'm really responsible, there is one last question to consider: What is the least violent, least destructive way of defending this good? What realistic means to defend it do I have available? The answer is necessary in deciding what to do.

Testing our anger by submitting it honestly to these questions, in the light of God and with trust, we will be able to handle the anger rationally, directing the energy it generates to accomplish good and not do evil. Someone else's counsel may be needed in doing this, since our strong feelings and the hurt we may have suffered can make it difficult.

Notice, too, that anger one feels toward oneself is usually no more justified than anger toward others. Usually it comes from pride. Meekness toward oneself is thus a necessary step in attaining meekness toward others. "*The meek are those who know how to suffer their neighbor and themselves.*" St. John of the Cross says.[28] We shall see more about this in the next section.

---

28. John of the Cross, "The Sayings of Light and Love," no. 164, *The Collected Works.*

With the grace of God, anger—except for certain involuntary first movements—can disappear little by little from our lives. That is a great benefit for us and for others. Anger will still be a source of a combative energy for justice and courage for truth, but no longer will it be a violent negative passion. And everyone will be better off for that.

MEEKNESS TOWARD ONE'S SELF

Regarding anger with ourselves, usually no more justified or productive than anger against others, let me simply quote some words of St. Francis de Sales. He speaks with much wisdom, realism, and humor, and it is worth reading the whole chapter on this subject in his *Introduction to the Devout Life*. Here is just a short passage, adapted to modern terminology:

> One important direction in which to exercise gentleness, is with respect to ourselves, never growing irritated with one's self or one's imperfections; for although it is but reasonable that we should be displeased and grieved at our own faults, yet ought we to guard against a bitter, angry, or peevish feeling about them. Many people fall into the error of being angry because they have been angry, vexed because

they have given way to vexation, thus keeping up a chronic state of irritation, which adds to the evil of what is past, and prepares the way for a fresh fall on the first occasion. Moreover, all this anger and irritation against one's self fosters pride, and springs entirely from self-love, which is disturbed and fretted by its own imperfection. . . .

So then, when you have fallen, lift up your heart in quietness, humbling yourself deeply before God by reason of your frailty, without marveling that you fell; there is no cause to marvel because weakness is weak, or infirmity infirm. Heartily lament that you should have offended God, and begin anew to cultivate the lacking grace, with a very deep trust in His Mercy, and with a bold, brave heart.[29]

How Is it that the Hearts of Men are Made Hard?

Acquiring evangelical meekness presupposes taking steps to ensure that our hearts do not harden. Scripture often denounces the hardening of hearts. What are its main causes? These include the following:

---

29. Francis de Sales, *Introduction to the Devout Life,* IX (San Francisco: Ignatius Press, 2015), EPUB.

First, pride. As humility leads to meekness, so does pride lead to hardening of the heart. This is especially so of the worst sort of pride, spiritual pride, which leads us to think ourselves better than others and attribute to ourselves the good things we accomplish. Pride in its various forms—the pride of knowing, of power, of intelligence—closes us off from others. I've already mentioned the hardness of the Pharisees in regard to the little people. If my degrees and my achievements lead me to judge others, I'd be better off without them.

Another fundamental source of hardness, according to Scripture, is lack of faith and trust in God. The fourth chapter of the letter to the Hebrews contains a commentary on Psalm 95, "*Today if you hear my voice harden not your hearts.*" The author of Hebrews clearly attributes this hardening to disbelief, a lack of trust in God and obedience to him, which is an obstacle to "*[entering] into my rest,*"[30] which God has prepared for his people. Lack of faith robs us of our peace, imprisons us in our fears and anxieties, and these then harden us and sometimes even make our hearts violent. Trust and hope do the reverse: softening, opening, making available, and welcoming others.

---

30. Ps 95:11.

A society that loses its faith, whose people no longer trust in God and where hope extends no further than the present life, is a society threatened by hardness. Where faith disappears, so do love and tenderness. Today's West is such a society.

Another cause of the hardening of heart against which Jesus strongly warns us is attachment to money and material wealth. Money can be a good servant, but it is a bad master. A heart ruled by love of money grows terribly hard. Consider the rich man in the parable in the Gospel of Luke.[31] He feasts daily in sumptuous clothes, unconcerned about the misery of poor Lazarus, who receives more compassion from the dogs who lick his wounds than from the rich man.

Attachment to money and avarice often come from fear of want, and lack of confidence in divine providence. This points to another cause of hardness: fear. Jesus warns of this in the Sermon on the Mount when he cautions against worrying about tomorrow in the knowledge that a heart preoccupied with worry will inevitably grow hard. "*Therefore do not be anxious about tomorrow, for tomorrow will be anxious for itself. Let the day's own trouble be sufficient for the day.*"[32]

---

31. Lk 16:19–31.
32. Mt 6:34.

Failure to accept suffering is another cause of hardening of heart, and a very common one. The management of suffering is a difficult and complex question, but it can at least be said that some people become humble, meek, or understanding of others through the experience of suffering while others become bitter, disappointed, even assertive and aggressive, as if they now had a right to make others suffer.

If suffering is not to become an occasion of hardness, it must be accepted and entrusted to God. In this way the suffering will acquire meaning as an occasion for the action of the Holy Spirit. We have no right to isolate ourselves and harden our hearts because of our sufferings. Instead we should open ourselves to God's consolation, the subject of the Beatitude to be considered next.

To repeat: the hardening of the heart I have been describing has its source in lack of faith and trust in God. Hence the insistence by Jesus on faith.

4

HAPPY ARE THOSE WHO HUNGER AND THIRST FOR JUSTICE. THEY WILL BE SATISFIED

Seek the LORD, all you humble of the land, who do
his commands; seek righteousness, seek humility.[1]

My soul thirsts for God, for the living God.
When shall I come and behold the face of God?[2]

With open mouth I pant, because I long
for thy commandments.[3]

Although it includes the usual sense of the term—
justice in human relations—justice, as it is understood

---

1. Zep 2:3.
2. Ps 42:2.
3. Ps 119:131

in the fourth Beatitude, has a much larger meaning. It is first of all a divine quality, of which the Bible often speaks: "*The LORD is just in all his ways, and kind in all his doings.*"[4]

God makes no exceptions but treats everyone with absolute equality. This divine justice is a requirement for humankind, which must stand before God in a relation of truth with no excuses. It is also a great support of faith to say God is just, meaning he is faithful, his love cannot deceive us, he understands what we are, our good will as well as our limits. "*I expect as much from God's justice as from His mercy,*" St. Thérèse of Lisieux says.[5]

To say God is just is also to affirm that, faithful to his love and his truth, he came to save. Justice and salvation are often associated—even synonymous: "*I have not hid thy saving help within my heart, I have spoken of thy faithfulness and thy salvation; I have not concealed thy steadfast love and thy faithfulness from the great congregation.*"[6] The just God is the God who justifies, the saving God. In Paul's letters, justice means justification, the free act through which God

---

4. Ps 145:17.

5. Thérèse of Lisieux, *General Correspondence Volume Two*, LT 226.

6. Ps 40:10.

gives his grace to sinners to transform them and clothe them in his own holiness.

THE DESIRE FOR HOLINESS

Understood thus, justice above all concerns a relationship with God. The just man, the "*tzadik*," has a true relationship with God, practices God's law with love, fully corresponding to what God expects of him. Justice in this sense is nothing other than holiness. But notice that biblical revelation, in the Old Testament but even more in the New, insists upon the very deep link between the truth of a relationship with God and justice toward one's neighbor. One could cite many passages, but consider only Isaiah's point that the fasting which pleases God aims "*to loose the bonds of wickedness, to undo the thongs of the yoke, to let the oppressed go free, and to break every yoke,*"[7] or chapter 25 of Matthew's Gospel on the last judgment, where Jesus declares that all we have done—or not done—to the least of our brothers and sisters has been done or not done to him. A relationship with God not rooted in justice and love toward one's

---

7. Is 58:6.

neighbor is an illusion, a lie. Justice toward others is the measure of our relationship with God. The two things are already inseparable in the Old Testament, and the link is made even stronger by the mystery of the Incarnation and the words of Jesus.

The primary aspect of the hunger and thirst for justice is then simply a true desire for holiness expressed as an inseparable love of God and of neighbor: "*I don't want to be a* saint by halves!" St. Thérèse of Lisieux said.[8]

This presupposes a sincere desire for conversion. Such desire is not sentimental but implies determination and courage to accept being formed by God in all the ways he employs in his merciful wisdom: his Word, life's events, the impact of others. Sometimes this will mean being like a rough mountain rock weathered by the rain, jostled right and left by other stones, until finally it becomes a smooth and polished pebble. Sometimes it will mean resembling a stone carved by a sculptor to fit for a niche for which it's intended. The thirst for justice is a thirst to let oneself be adjusted to God and to others, consenting to what can be a painful process.

---

8. Thérèse of Lisieux, *Story of a Soul*, loc. 960 of 6450.

DESIRE SALVATION FOR ALL

In another sense, the thirst for justice is the ardent desire that God's salvation be realized for everybody.

One of the most beautiful passages in the Old Testament is Isaiah chapters 61 and 62 making it clear that the justice desired and expected is infinitely richer than justice in social relations—although these cannot be neglected—but is the divine work of salvation in favor of humankind, here hailed in splendid terms as a wedding between bride and groom:

> I will greatly rejoice in the LORD, my soul shall exult in my God; for he has clothed me with the garments of salvation, he has covered me with the robe of righteousness, as a bridegroom decks himself with a garland, and as a bride adorns herself with her jewels. For as the earth brings forth its shoots, and as a garden causes what is sown in it to spring up, so the Lord GOD will cause righteousness and praise to spring forth before all the nations.[9]

> You shall no more be termed Forsaken, and your land shall no more be termed Desolate; but you shall be called My delight is in her, and your land Married;

9. Is 61:10–11.

for the LORD delights in you, and your land shall be married. For as a young man marries a virgin, so shall your sons marry you, and as the bridegroom rejoices over the bride, so shall your God rejoice over you.[10]

In this context, hunger and thirst for justice signify the desire that the Kingdom of God come in all its glory. Scripture gives this its ultimate expression in the Book of Revelation:

The Spirit and the Bride say, "Come." And let him who hears say, "Come." And let him who is thirsty come, let him who desires take the water of life without price.[11]

And a few lines later this is summed up by the "*Maranatha, Come Lord Jesus!*" that we recite at every Eucharist.

Hunger and thirst for justice, desire for the Kingdom, far from being passive waiting, are actively expressed in announcing the good news of the gospel and the work of transforming society to which each of us is called. Perseverance in prayer—lovingly asking God to advance this time when all this will be accomplished—is part of it. The Church's prayer, like that of

10. Is 62:4–5.
11. Rv 22:17.

the Virgin Mary at Cana, has the power to speed up the hour of grace, as Peter suggests in his second letter: *"What sort of persons ought you to be in lives of holiness and godliness, waiting for and hastening the coming of the day of God."*[12]

As Isaiah says in the chapters mentioned, having a hunger and thirst for justice involves calling upon God not to delay in fulfilling his promises.

> For Zion's sake I will not keep silent, and for Jerusalem's sake I will not rest, until her vindication goes forth as brightness, and her salvation as a burning torch.[13]

> Upon your walls, O Jerusalem, I have set watchmen; all the day and all the night they shall never be silent. You who put the LORD in remembrance, take no rest, and give him no rest until he establishes Jerusalem and makes it a praise in the earth.[14]

God himself asks us not to leave him in peace as long as his promises of salvation are not entirely fulfilled.

We find this moving passage in the Lamentations of Jeremiah after the destruction of Jerusalem:

---

12. 2 Pt 3:11–12.

13. Is 62:1.

14. Is 62:6–7.

Cry aloud to the Lord! O daughter of Zion! Let tears stream down like a torrent day and night! Give yourself no rest, your eyes no respite! Arise, cry out in the night, at the beginning of the watches! Pour out your heart like water before the presence of the Lord! Lift your hands to him for the lives of your children, who faint for hunger at the head of every street.[15]

Here again are those tears of compassion and supplication that we found in the Beatitude of the mourning.

Thus one of the most authentic expressions of a thirst for justice is incessant prayer. We are reminded of this by the conclusion of the parable of the widow who finally obtained justice by persisting in seeking it from a judge otherwise heedless of God and man. Jesus concludes this parable exhorting us to "*pray without ceasing*" with these words:

Will not God vindicate his elect, who cry to him day and night? Will he delay long over them? I tell you, he will vindicate them speedily. Nevertheless, when the Son of Man comes, will he find faith on the earth?[16]

---

15. Lam 2:18–19.
16. Lk 18:7–8.

Asking God to do justice for us should not be understood as calling upon him to punish those who harm us but rather to speed our personal conversion: Lord, it's not just for me to love you so little while you deserve to be loved so much, or to love my neighbor so little when he has such a need for love. Do me justice! Convert me and transform my heart, filling it with love for you and others.

THE DESIRE FOR TRUTH

The thirst for justice is a thirst for conversion, for interior transformation. It is not so much personal perfection that we seek as a will to respond to God's desire. It accompanies the tears of repentance to which we referred in speaking of the second Beatitude.

It appears to me that an important expression of this thirst for conversion is the desire for truth: refusing all forms of illusion and self-deception, all lies to ourselves, all compromises and "close enoughs" in our relationship with God and others. We must place our lives in their entirety under the light of God and have the courage of truth. Shortly before her death, the little Thérèse of Lisieux said: "*I never sought anything but the truth!*"[17] It

---

17. Thérèse of Lisieux, *Conversations*, September 30.

is clear from experience that people who make the most progress in the spiritual life are not necessarily at the beginning the most virtuous or most devout. They are those who most insist on being honest with themselves and take concrete steps to be truthful with God: prayer, reflection, serious reading of Scripture, spiritual direction, retreats, and so on. The problem is not so much with our wounds or our faults but our failure to face up to them in the light of God.

To insist on truth takes for granted the poorness of heart and humility of which the first Beatitude speaks. Humility extends a welcome to truth and accepts being troubled by it when that is necessary. Pride is the opposite and is one of the principal causes of blindness. Welcoming the truth requires submitting oneself to something other than ourselves, something that surpasses us. But only truth makes us free, as Jesus says in the Gospel of John.[18]

WHAT IS MY DEEPEST DESIRE?

The fourth Beatitude points to a question: What is my deepest desire?

---

18. Jn 8:32.

Hunger and thirst are images of desire for in what is most vital and essential. It is good to put this question to one's heart: What is my deepest desire? What do I really hunger and thirst for? What desire is the principle of unity for my life?

It is natural that one have several desires, yet this can be a source of interior division and the accomplishment of some of our desires can lead us to an impasse or deceive us. St. Paul speaks of the need for a certain filtering or discernment, to distinguish those that come from the "flesh" (our wounded psyches) from those that come from the "spirit" (our authentic aspirations for what is really good for us and the promptings of the Holy Spirit).

But among all our desires one is dominant in that it gathers together and unifies all the others. We find in one of the Psalms this wonderful prayer: "*Teach me thy way, O Lord, that I may walk in thy truth; unite my heart to fear thy name.*"[19] And Jesus says: "*He who does not gather with me scatters.*"[20] In failing to direct their desire toward God, people risk 'scattering' themselves.

Fortunate are those whose most profound desire is not confined to some human ambition but is centered

---

19. Ps 86:11.
20. Mt 12:30.

upon a desire for sainthood, the desire to please God and do his will, to love God and neighbor with all the strength of their hearts. They will receive what they desire and will be fulfilled.

But how is a desire for sainthood, for God, kept alive? For it can fade, as in the case of religious who ardently desired holiness during their novitiate years and, four decades later, desire only a kind of soft mediocrity. The question is complex, but I believe one of the main reasons for the loss of this desire is a lack of faithfulness to prayer; whereas contact with God sustains and feeds this desire—contact kept up by reading, by sharing with other believers, and by acts of love and acceptance of suffering.

Another explanation for the extinguishing of this desire is discouragement arising from the repeated experience of one's misery and poverty that can sometimes drive a person to abandon the ambition of becoming holy. Here the remedy is humility, recognition of one's powerlessness together with audacious hope and blind faith in the mercy and power of God.

The fundamental process of the spiritual life is a purification of desire in its object and its foundation: on the one hand, in order that the soul's desires be gathered together and unified with the desire for God, little by little putting aside any aspiration that is outside of the divine will; on the other hand, hoping against hope (cf. Rom 4:18), so that this desire be based not on our human capabilities, but solely on the mercy of God. The more miserable and poor I see myself to be, the more I dare to look for fulfillment with faith in the infinite mercy of God.

This desire is not always felt, of course, and that isn't something to worry about. Yes, it would be grand to be in a state of permanent ecstasy. Everything would be so easy then. But it is neither possible nor desirable. One of the familiar trials of the spiritual life is to experience spells of dryness in which one is poor and without desire, able only to offer to God a humble good will. It's enough. This experience of poverty purifies desire and causes it to be founded only on God.

May the Thirst of Jesus Become our Thirst

Still, it is good to examine ourselves concerning thirst and know how to change course and revive our desire. But we must also realize that there is a thirst more ardent than all human desire. I mean God's thirst, the thirst of Jesus himself. God thirsts to love us and give himself to us. "*Give me a drink,*" Jesus said to the Samaritan woman,[21] and before he died he said: "*I thirst.*"[22] "*[God] has no need of our works, but only of our love,*" St. Thérèse of Lisieux said.[23] This thirst that Jesus expresses was the inspiration of the life of Mother Teresa.

Our desire for God is nothing compared to his desire for us. He loves us and desires us infinitely more than we can desire and love him. Our desire can have highs and lows, but God's desire to love us can never diminish or be extinguished. Despite our infidelity and lukewarmness, God will always want to love us, to give himself to us, to save us.

And it is this desire of his that can awaken and stimulate ours. We must believe in it, offer ourselves to it, without ever becoming discouraged in the face of our destitution. We must believe that God wants to wed us in spite of our ugliness and, believing, allow him do it. It is he whose gaze will make us worthy and clothe us in beauty.

If we let ourselves be visited by and wed to the Lord, he will make us part of his thirst. It is wonderful to

---

21. Jn 4:7.

22. Jn 19:28.

23. Thérèse of Lisieux, *Story of a Soul*, loc. 3324 of 6450.

notice how in the lives of saints human hearts are consumed by a thirst communicated to them by God—a
thirst for love, a thirst for the Kingdom, a desire to save
souls more ardent than the maddest of human passions.
Thérèse of Lisieux lived through this at the age of 14,
just after her healing at Christmas, and this experience
guided her during her life at Carmel.

> He [Jesus] made me a fisher of souls. I experienced a
> great desire to work for the conversion of sinners, a
> desire that I hadn't felt so intensely before. . . . The
> cry of Jesus on the cross sounded continually in my
> heart: "I thirst!" These words ignited within me an
> unknown and very living fire. I wanted to give my
> Beloved to drink and I felt myself consumed with a
> *thirst for souls. As yet* it was not the souls of priests that
> attracted me, but those of *great sinners*; I *burned* with
> the desire to snatch them from the eternal flames.[24]

Let us ask Jesus to communicate his desires to us,
and come to satisfy them. Then we shall be full beyond
all measuring.

Notice, too, that the more we go thirsting to
drink at the fountain of the heart of God, the more

---

24. Thérèse of Lisieux, *Story of a Soul*, loc. 1990 and 1995–1998 of 6450.

we become fountains for others. Jesus promises this in John's Gospel.

> On the last day of the feast, the great day, Jesus stood up and proclaimed, "If any one thirst, let him come to me and drink. He who believes in me, as the scripture has said, 'Out of his heart shall flow rivers of living water.'"[25]

In the same way, the more we hunger for Jesus, and for the Eucharist in particular, and the more we live for him, the more we shall be able to become food for others. We are called to respond to people's hunger and thirst, which is so great today. When faced with the famished crowd, Jesus says to his disciples, "*You give them something to eat.*"[26]

REPAIR THE FUNDAMENTAL INJUSTICE THAT LEADS OTHERS ASTRAY

The greatest injustice in all history is ultimately that God is not loved as much as he should be, that he is so forgotten, so neglected—that human beings take so

---

25. Jn 7:37–38.
26. Lk 9:13.

little note of their creator and savior, that those invited to the wedding feast find a thousand excuses for not responding to the call.[27] So many passages in the Bible express God's suffering because of his misunderstood love. Recall Jeremiah's words: "*They have forsaken me, the fountain of living waters, and hewed out cisterns for themselves, broken cisterns, that can hold no water.*"[28] The words of Hosea: "*When Israel was a child, I loved him, and out of Egypt I called my son. The more I called them, the more they went from me.*"[29] Recall, too, Jesus' tears shed over the holy city: "*O Jerusalem, Jerusalem, killing the prophets and stoning those who are sent to you! How often would I have gathered your children together as a hen gathers her brood under her wings, and you would not!*"[30]

At the deepest level, hunger and thirst for justice arise from suffering in face of the failure to love God. Personal misfortune is not what most pains God's friends, but the fact that God is not loved. The psalmist put it this way: "*My eyes shed streams of tears, because*

---

27. See the parable of the Wedding Banquet, Mt 22:1–14.
28. Jer 2:13.
29. Hos 11:1–2.
30. Mt 23:37.

men do not keep thy law."[31] And St. Francis of Assisi said, "*Love isn't loved!*" We express our hunger and thirst for God to be finally recognized and embraced for what he is every time we recite the Our Father: "*Hallowed be thy name, thy kingdom come.*"

In the end, then, to be hungry and thirsty for justice means ardently desiring that God be better known and loved. It means desiring to respond to ingratitude by a surfeit of love. It means wanting to embrace God, love God, and trust God to make up for all those who do not embrace, love, and trust him.

---

31. Ps 119:136.

5

HAPPY ARE
THE MERCIFUL
FOR THEY SHALL
OBTAIN MERCY

Be kind to one another, tenderhearted,
forgiving one another, as God in Christ forgave you.[1]

The fifth Beatitude has a unique structure unlike any
of the other's: the promised reward (mercy) is identical
to what it calls us to do. But there is a similar structure in
other Gospel passages, especially chapter 6 of St. Luke,
which is also one of Jesus' invitations to practice mercy.

Be merciful, even as your Father is merciful. Judge
not, and you will not be judged; condemn not, and

---

1. Eph 4:32.

you will not be condemned; forgive, and you will be forgiven; give and it will be given to you; good measure, pressed down, shaken together, running over, will be put into your lap. For the measure you give will be the measure you get back.[2]

This expresses a fundamental truth, not about punishment and reward but about something more profound, an essential law of the human condition and as rigorous as a law of the physical world, we might say.

There is a very deep connection, emphasized in Scripture, between one's relationship with God and one's relationship with others. Closing one's heart to a brother means automatically closing one's heart to God and his grace, while opening one's heart to another is a sure way of opening one's heart to God and his abundant blessings. The divine blessing will be measured out to me according to my attitude toward my neighbor.

The good I do another will return to me as blessing; the bad—acted out, spoken, or even merely thought—will sooner or later come back to me. This is absolutely certain. To curse someone is to curse one's self. To detest or hate someone is to destroy one's self. We shall always be the victims of the bad we do to others.

2. Lk 6:36–38.

Here is an inexorable law of life, and it would be better that we take account of it and so live fully than that,
as it were, we destroy ourselves. It resembles the law of
gravity: if we respect it, we can put satellites in orbit, but
if we don't, we crash to the ground. I can testify that any
time I've judged someone else, I've soon enough been
repaid by some sorrowful experience of my own misery.
This hasn't entirely cured me, but I hope that will come.

The fifth Beatitude expresses a particular aspect of
this law. The more I show mercy to my brother, the more
merciful God will be toward me. "*Love covers a multitude of sins,*" St. Peter says.[3] According to St. Thérèse of
Lisieux,[4] this is an inexhaustible source of the mercy we
need so badly, placed at our disposal by Jesus.

He insists on the essential link between being forgiven by God and forgiving one's neighbor at several
places in the Gospel. As the parable of the Unforgiving
Servant in Matthew's Gospel teaches,[5] God is ready to
forgive our greatest debts, on the condition that we be

---

3. 1 Pt 4:8. "Above all hold unfailing your love for one another, since
love covers a multitude of sins."

4. "Remembering that 'charity covers a multitude of sins,' I draw from
this rich mine that Jesus has opened up before me." Thérèse of Lisieux,
Story of a Soul, loc. 3914 of 6450.

5. Mt 18:23–25.

ready to forgive the debts, often so tiny, of our brothers and sisters who wrong us.

This parable is set in a context. Peter approaches the Lord with a question: "*How often shall my brother sin against me, and I forgive him? As many as seven times?*" No doubt Peter expected praise from Jesus: "You're a great guy for forgiving seven times. Some never forgive, others only two or three times. Fantastic, you make it seven. I've done well to make you the head of my apostles." Poor Peter! Jesus' reaction wasn't what he expected but this: "*I do not say to you seven times, but seventy times seven.*"[6] God's forgiveness of us is limitless; ours should be too. Be merciful as your Father is merciful.

The fifth Beatitude concerns all aspects of mercy, of course, not just forgiveness. It applies to those forms of the goodness, love, benevolence, patience, and mutual support to which the New Testament so often summons us. Nothing draws God's grace into our lives more than the humble, patient charity we practice toward others. Forgiveness is one of the highest forms of mercy and also one of the hardest. But it is worth the effort to extend it more widely.

------

6. Mt 18:21–22.

The Source of Forgiveness

Forgiveness is difficult, sometimes heroic, but it is indispensable. Without forgiveness, evil multiplies ceaselessly. Only the courage to forgive puts an end to evil's growth.

Moreover, the pain someone else has caused me can only be completely cured by my forgiving that person. We see victims all around us these days. And we work hard to understand them, embrace them, encourage them to express their suffering, their anger, and their sense of injustice; we strive to help them obtain recognition and recompense for the wrong they've suffered. And all this is very good. But sometimes we overlook helping them to understand that, unless they forgive the people who have hurt them, they will never fully recover from the pain.

God's love is powerful enough to heal everything, but you must find the courage to decide to pass through the "narrow gate" of forgiveness. This choice is more demanding than the spontaneous reaction of resentment and accusation, but it is a decision in favor of true life.

Father, Forgive Them . . .

There is something that can sometimes make the difficult path of forgiveness easier. People have told me, "I couldn't say 'I forgive,' but the words of Jesus on his cross 'Father, forgive them, they don't know what they do,' came more easily."

There is an important truth here. Only God can truly forgive, because only he can heal the evil that has been done, and revive what is dead. The ultimate source of forgiveness is the merciful heart of the Father, and we must turn to this source to be able to forgive, seeking there in humility and faith for the grace to be able to pardon, and embracing the Father's merciful love in our own hearts.

Jesus' words invite us to turn to the Father first of all. They also help us realize that human beings truly do not know what they are doing, fail to comprehend the evil of which they are the authors. It is deeply moving to hear Jesus pardon those who made him suffer rather than condemning them. Repeating his words helps us enter into his interior disposition, his openness to the Father and his benevolence toward humankind, and this helps our human hearts embrace the grace of pardon.

Sometimes of course we are a long while obtaining this grace. The first step is to want it and ask for it. But much time can elapse between the decision to forgive and complete peace. There are high periods and low ones, moments when anger returns in full force. This is normal, but if we persevere in a determined, patient way, one day the grace of full healing will come.

Forgiveness, Act of Faith and Hope

It is very helpful to the decision to forgive to understand that forgiveness is an act not only of charity but also of faith and hope.

Often we encounter a grave obstacle to forgiveness in the feeling that the evil committed is irreparable, precisely because someone—the guilty party, the victim, I, somebody I love—has been changed irreparably: something has been broken in his or her life that can never be fixed. Things will never again be as they were before. Humanly speaking, this feeling is understandable, and it makes forgiveness nearly impossible.

But faith tells us that God is able to heal all wounds: "*Where sin increased, grace abounded all the more.*"[7] It

_____

7. Rom 5:20.

tells us: "*The sufferings of this present time are not worth comparing with the glory that is to be revealed to us*."[8] It tells us, in the words of the second Beatitude: "*Blessed are those who mourn, for they shall be comforted.*"[9]

If we have faith and hope that, whatever the evil, God can make a still greater good of it—that wounds inflicted by the actions of another will not only be healed one day but will become a source of life and happiness far exceeding the evil that was done—forgiving will be easier. No longer do we have grounds for holding grudges against those who have wronged us if faith and hope testify that God will give us some greater good than the evil we have suffered. Rather than a human guarantee, we have God's Word for this; and the central affirmation of our Christian faith is Christ's resurrection testifying conclusively that death can be transformed into an abundance of life.

There are many witnesses to the truth of all this— many people who have experienced grievous suffering caused by others yet found the strength to forgive and in doing so attained a grandeur of soul, a fullness of charity, and a freedom to love far greater than they would have known had everything in their lives been

8. Rom 8:18.
9. Mt 5:4.

easy. To take just one of the countless examples: Maiti Girtanner, a young French Resistance fighter whose life was broken by Nazi torture, encountered her torturer many years later and was able to assure him of her forgiveness.[10]

The faith and hope that underlie forgiveness encompass not only our wounds but also the person we forgive. Refusing to forgive signifies that I identify this person with the evil he or she has committed and judge him or her to be irremediably bad. But have we a right to do this? No one is ever reducible simply to his or her bad acts.

Our churches are full of the images of saints with halos, flowing robes, and angelic visages. But how many of them were once murderers, adulterers, or people like St. Augustine who made their mother weep for thirty years—great sinners until the grace of conversion touched them? To refuse to forgive is, in a way, to despair of the conversion of someone who has made us suffer. But God never gives up on anyone and always looks for the conversion of the criminal. Should we not imitate him?

To forgive one's enemy is to make an act of hope that the enemy will undergo conversion. There's no

---

10. See "The Return of a Soul to a Torturer," *L'Osservatore Romano,* December 12, 2012, *http://www.osservatoreromano.va/en/news/the-return-of-a-soul-to-a-torturer.*

denying this person made me suffer, and may have committed a very serious sin, but I can't condemn him or her, inasmuch as I hope for the conversion of his or her heart.

Hope contains an enormous power. I love the image St. Paul uses in chapter 12 of the Letter to the Romans. Inviting us not to repay evil with evil, not to exact our own version of justice, but to put things in God's hands and love our enemies, he writes: "*If your enemy is hungry, feed him; if he is thirsty, give him drink; for by so doing you will heap burning coals upon his head. Do not be overcome by evil, but overcome evil with good.*"[11]

What does Paul mean when he speaks of "heap[ing] burning coals upon" an enemy's head? Does this refer to God's punishment of destroying the guilty, in the manner sought by James and John, who wanted divine fire to fall on a Samaritan village that didn't welcome them?[12] (For this they were severely reprimanded by Jesus.) No, it means something very different, as Father Joseph-Marie Verlinde points out in a homily.

> In reality, the Apostle is making an allusion to a met-
> allurgical process used in biblical times. The ore was

---

11. Rom 12:20–21.
12. Lk 9:51–55.

placed into an oven over a layer of hot coals. Then another layer of burning coals was heaped on top of it, in order to melt the metal and purify it.

In other words, charitable works, good actions accomplished in the fire of the Holy Spirit, which Saint Paul invites us to perform freely for our enemies, have the goal of making their hearts "melt," so that they are purified from the dregs of malice that prevent them from conversion.

We find the same expression in one of St. Catherine of Siena's letters in which she invites us to practice patience toward those who wrong us: "*When you return good for evil you not only prove your own virtue, but often you send out coals ablaze with charity that will melt hatred and bitterness from the heart and mind of the wrathful, even turning their hatred to benevolence.*"[13]

There is much power in forgiveness and mercy; this is much more than a private affair. Every act of forgiving, one might say, adds its bit to the fire of the Holy Spirit gathering over the person forgiven, and when there is enough of it, this fire will descend and make his or her heart melt. Each act of mercy helps prepare a Pentecost!

---

13. Catherine of Siena. *The Dialogue*, trans. Suzanne Noffke, OP (New York: Paulist Press, 1980), p. 39.

The same interpretation applies to Jesus' words in the Gospel: "*Whatever you bind on earth shall be bound in heaven, and whatever you loose on earth shall be loosed in heaven.*"[14] If I am courageous enough to release someone from vengeance on earth by forgiving him or her, it has immense repercussions in heaven: a Pentecost, a powerful outpouring of the Spirit is prepared, and one day it will happen. When or how is not for us to say, but our hope is certain. And "*hope does not disappoint us,*"[15] St. Paul says.

Every time we exercise mercy, goodness, patience, or forgiveness, we hasten along the coming reign of God, that immense outpouring of love which will transform human hearts.

FORGIVENESS MAKES US FREE

Forgiving others also possesses another important property: it makes us free. Obviously it is good for the person forgiven, but it does even more good to the one who forgives, helping him or her find freedom and peace, which are priceless!

---

14. Mt 18:18.
15. Rom 5:5.

Not forgiving means remaining trapped in the past. If I suffered something twenty years ago and haven't forgiven the party responsible for it, I am in effect chained to something that happened long ago, and unable fully to enjoy the beauty of what is given me today. Some part of me is closed to the blessings of the present because it is imprisoned in the past.

Once, while visiting a parish mission in Italy, I met a woman, then more than ninety years old, who was eaten up by resentment toward the nuns who had taught her when she was twelve. It was her main topic of conversation, which she kept coming back to again and again. I couldn't judge this woman. But how sad it was to see someone so trapped in her own past at an age when it is a time to concentrate on preparing joyfully for one's encounter with God.

Refusing to forgive means hanging on to thoughts and feelings of resentment, anger, and bitterness in our hearts. These things take up our energy, and prevent us from being open to the richness of life and becoming the best version of ourselves. Here is a form of emotional addiction that causes us to think as much about someone we hate as about someone we love. And the hatred makes us resemble the hated person; it disfigures us! We must free ourselves from all this that imprisons and poisons us, and we must do it as soon as we can, at whatever the cost. Only forgiveness will suffice to accomplish that.[16]

FORGIVE ALL DEBTS

In speaking of forgiveness, Jesus often uses the image of a debt. One example is found in the parable of the unforgiving debtor from the eighteenth chapter of St. Matthew's Gospel, and another in the Our Father, where we ask God to forgive us our debts as we forgive our debtors.

---

16. These are the words of Jorje Valls, who spent twenty years in Fidel Castro's jails, quoted in an editorial in *Ouest France* of 10/31/2015. "*I have never in my entire life been as free as when I was in prison. Why? Because defeated, humiliated, famished, subjected to a pace designed to make us lose all our bearings, there was one thing that remained deep within me, one thing that others couldn't take, an indestructible thing, the only thing that I could keep: my dignity, my interior freedom. This made me see others, the prisoners, my compatriots or the guards, the torturers, with another view. I learned, over the years, that it was this view that counted, that made me live. This is what made me forgive my persecutors. It was this forgiveness that I taught to my companions in misery. I learned and said over twenty years to those around me that it was the only important, essential thing. If I hadn't forgiven, I would have become like my persecutors, that is to say, full of hate. Forgiveness prevents us from becoming rabid beasts. Forgiveness puts us above woe, hate, disdain. My enemy became my brother.*"

This metaphor of debt highlights an obvious fact on the psychological level, and one recognized in everyday speech. When one person wrongs another, the spontaneous reaction is, "You'll pay for this!" If someone does me a wrong, I consider that person to owe me something, and therefore I have a right to claim reparation, even a right to revenge, so that he or she will suffer as I did. But this reaction is infantile. We do not rebuild what was destroyed in us by destroying the other. That just increases the evil, spreading it while making it grow in ourselves.

To be sure, there is a legitimate desire for justice behind this way of reacting. The difficulty is that we too often want to do justice ourselves, strictly according to the measure of our feelings, and so we do more bad than good. We invest all our negative feelings into the effort—our anger and resentment, our dissatisfaction with life—and in doing so we drive away any possibility of reconciliation and love. "Settling accounts" with someone is rarely done in a just and equitable way.

How much better would it be, as the gospel invites us, to put our cause in God's hands, leave the re-establishing of justice to him (there will be less collateral damage that way) and renounce our demands.

We tend to retain vivid memories of the injuries we've suffered, as if we were keeping accounts and expecting some day to present bills to the guilty parties and demand compensation. Meantime our attitude to such people might be summed up as: "Watch out, it's all going into the book, and one day you'll pay for it."

Not forgiving means keeping many such invoices, carefully recorded, up our sleeves. Yet this wad of bills invariably ends by poisoning people's lives, feeding bitterness, reproach, and expectations of repayment that generally go unrealized. What was lost can't be restored as we wish: our demands swell out of all proportion; we find ourselves in a dependent relationship with the supposedly (but perhaps not truly) guilty party, cut off from true freedom, which can only be regained by throwing away all those invoices—"forgiving the debts," as the Our Father asks us to do.

GETTING OUT OF THE TIT-FOR-TAT MENTALITY

When someone does us harm, we judge that he owes us reparation. This gives us a right, and with that right comes a certain power over the one who has harmed us. But much the same situation may arise when we do good to someone. Suppose I do you some service: now you owe me something in return. Here, too, there is a certain legitimacy in feeling this way. Yet there also is a good chance that our expectation will become an obsession, a dependence, a demand that is impossible to satisfy and is bound to leave us disappointed. If, for example, parents expect their children to be grateful in proportion to what the parents have done for them, they will be very disappointed indeed.

Often we suppose that the good we do for others gives us particular rights over them. But this is a huge mistake. We should do good freely, without impairing our freedom.

This tendency to think and act with the mentality of exchange or contract has a certain validity, of course—for example, in a context of law—and must be respected accordingly. It is natural that someone who has suffered an injustice should receive reparations and seek them in court if it comes to that. It is also natural that someone who has done a job should be paid, and if necessary he or she also can go to court to enforce that payment. And in a marriage, if one partner does all the giving and the other all the receiving, without a mutual exchange of affection and service, the 'giving' partner may quite reasonably become annoyed and seek a discussion focused on making some adjustments.

But the logic of reciprocity of exchange cannot extend to the whole field of human relations. It has its limits, and it will never be a hundred percent perfect. We have to be satisfied even when reciprocity fails and we have the feeling of being treated unjustly. Above all, we need to recognize when the time has come to put aside this exchange-based logic and enter into the economy of free giving—the only logic that permits the blossoming of love and the realization of true happiness. This in the end is the attitude that reigns in the Kingdom, where the only rule is love.

No One Owes Me Anything

Here is why the gospel invites us not to submit claims for the payment of debts but to forgive them. If someone has wronged you or you've done somebody some good, don't think they owe you something. Renounce your claim. Learn to love without expecting anything in return. Jesus' words—strong to the point of being scandalous—aren't a demand that we do something bizarre but an attempt to extricate us from exchange-based logic so that we can finally be free to love:

You have heard that it was said, 'An eye for an eye
and a tooth for a tooth.' But I say to you, do not
resist one who is evil. But if any one strikes you on
the right cheek, turn to him the other also; and if
any one would sue you and take your coat, let him
have your cloak as well; and if any one forces you
to go one mile, go with him two miles.[17]

Shocking? Jesus' words point the way to freedom.
Put aside the calculating and account keeping, the fears
and defense mechanisms, the sterile demands. Taste the
joy of truly, freely loving.

So why is it that we get nervous at the thought
of giving up this mercantile logic of debts and rights?
Why so much resistance to putting it aside?

The answer, I think, is that the fear arises from a
lack of faith. We want ironclad guarantees. We want
to be certain of having everything we think happiness requires instead of trusting God for that. And
the exchange-based system allows us to have a certain
power over others, to control them. This tendency
is deeply rooted. But we cannot truly love without
renouncing all efforts to control or manipulate the
other or have any sort of claim upon him or her.

---

17. Mt 5:38–41.

We are afraid to forgive debts because we are afraid of finding ourselves wiped out, unable to get what we need to be happy. But the math doesn't work. This is what the gospel means by "saving" one's life and thereby losing it. For it leads to looking to others to give us the security, peace, and happiness that only God can give us.

If, on the other hand, we trust God's word we can forgive all our debts with the peace of mind that comes from looking to God for everything that gives value to life. God is faithful, and he returns to us five times over what we give up for him. "*The Lord is my shepherd, I shall not want.*"[18]

Thus, to be free and happy, we must have the courage to tell ourselves "No one owes me anything." Not those who harmed me, because I've forgiven them, and not those to whom I've done good, because I want to love them freely. We must burn all of those invoices we're prepared and forgive all those debts. Here is one of the most important forms of that poverty of spirit to which the Beatitudes summon us. The Lord tells us: "*Whoever of you does not renounce all that he has cannot be my disciple.*"[19]

At the top of the list of things calling for renunciation (and sometimes hardest to renounce) are our

---

18. Ps 23:1.
19. Lk 14:33.

supposed "rights" over others. But the courage to renounce will release us from the trap of demands and claims, and we will enter into a world of freedom and love where happiness lies: there is, after all, more joy in giving than in receiving.

It is a surprising lesson, taught by experience, that the more we make demands on others, the less we receive, while the less we require of others, the more we receive from them in the end. Pursuing a mercantile logic in human relations introduces a kind of violence into relationships. Demanding too much justice sooner or later leads to injustice. Justice unaccompanied by mercy sooner or later becomes injustice.

A Short Story of a Couple's Forgiveness

Here is a story that illustrates what I've been saying.

During a retreat I was preaching some years ago, a woman came to see me who had great difficulty forgiving. Her husband had cheated on her years before, and although the episode hadn't lasted long, it hurt her deeply. That's understandable: whatever people may think these days, adultery is a grave sin that betrays the bond of marital intimacy, and it's very painful for the party who is wronged. But despite what she had suffered, this woman, a practicing Christian, felt she had to forgive her husband.

"I've read all the books on forgiveness," she told me, "but I'm just not getting there."

I could see where the problem was. Not forgiving her husband offered two great advantages. First, she was the victim, the innocent saint, and he was the sinner. To forgive would require a lot of humility on her part. It would mean giving up her position of superiority and placing herself on the same level with him: both of them poor sinners, he sinning against her and she with her own faults, perhaps less obvious but just as real as his, yet remaining together, each of them embracing the other with his and her limitations.

Second, she had difficulty renouncing the authority over her husband that his wrongdoing gave her. As matters stood, she felt justified in reproaching him, keeping an eye on him, and exercising a hold on him. Forgiveness would mean renouncing all that control and power. But although painful, in the end it is a source of peace and happiness, a way of freedom. Release the other from the yoke I make him wear and suddenly I am released from the destructive attitude that was smothering me. "*Is this not the fast that I choose: to loose the bonds of wickedness, to undo the thongs of the yoke, to let the oppressed go free, and to break every yoke?*"[20]

How rewarding it is to understand and practice this biblical wisdom today!

One final remark on forgiveness: St. Paul offers this counsel: "*Owe no one anything, except to love one another; for he who loves his neighbor has fulfilled the law*."[21] Do not ground your relationships in debts and demands, rights and duties, but in the generosity of love. This is how the Kingdom will become present among you.

EXERCISING MERCY DOES US GOOD

The exercise of mercy does us good. Consider more deeply this magnificent text from chapter 58 of Isaiah, which we read at the beginning of Lent:

> Is not this the fast that I choose: to loose the bonds of wickedness, to undo the thongs of the yoke, to let the oppressed go free, and to break every yoke? Is it not to share your bread with the hungry, and bring

20. Is 58:6.
21. Rom 13:8.

the homeless poor into your house; when you see the naked, to cover him, and not to hide yourself from your own flesh?

Then shall your light break forth like the dawn, and your healing shall spring up speedily; your righteousness shall go before you, the glory of the LORD shall be your rear guard. Then you shall cry, and he will say, *Here I am.*

If you take away from the midst of you the yoke, the pointing of the finger, and speaking wickedness, if you pour yourself out for the hungry and satisfy the desire of the afflicted, then shall your light rise in the darkness and your gloom be as the noonday.

And the LORD will guide you continually, and satisfy your desire with good things, and make your bones strong; and you shall be like a watered garden, like a spring of water, whose waters fail not.[22]

The sheer quantity of promises and abundance of blessings in this passage for those who practice love of neighbor is remarkable. The passage touched St. Thérèse of Lisieux deeply, and she often cited it to her novices. In a helpful commentary, her sister Céline notes that Thérèse interpreted the phrase "*let*

---

22. Is 58:6–11.

the oppressed go free" as meaning that, hearing someone speak of a sister's faults, one should never add to
the recitation of failings but, without being untruthful
should add one of her good qualities to the list.[23]

The words "*when you see the naked, to cover him*"[24]
can be understood along the same lines: If someone's
poverty and misery are evident, don't make matters
worse, but clothe this person in a cloak of mercy.

It's a good idea to reflect on this today, when the
media give a lot of attention to poverty, frailty, and
human weakness, and in doing so indulge popular
voyeurism. Of course complicity in injustice and
unhealthy, silent complacency are unacceptable, but so
is destroying the reputations of people or communities
(something easily done) or inviting others to gawk at
them. Someone moved to expose the sin and weakness of others can be sure of someday having his or her
own misery exposed to the sunlight. We will be treated
exactly as we have treated others. Certain journalists,
like all the rest of us, would do well to think about this.

---

23. Thérèse of Lisieux and Sister Geneviève, *Conseils et souvenirs*, pp. 93–96.
24. Cf. Mt 25:36, 44.

6

HAPPY ARE THE PURE OF HEART

Having purified your souls by your obedience to
the truth for a sincere love of the brethren, love one
another earnestly from the heart. You have been
born anew, not of perishable seed but of imperish-
able, through the living and abiding word of God.[1]

The purity of heart of which the sixth Beatitude
speaks has magnificent consequences: "*To the pure all
things are pure,*" Paul says in his letter to Titus.[2] Purity
of heart illuminates life, and transforms one's way of
thinking. Purity and impurity are not in things but in
one's way of seeing them.

A beautiful promise accompanies purity: God
himself. And not only will the pure of heart see him

1. 1 Pt 1:22–23.
2. Tit 1:15.

some day in paradise—a vision that will fill them with happiness—but here and now, in the recognition of God's action in their lives. There is nothing greater than to know God. "*And this is eternal life, that they know thee the only true God.*"[3] When people think of God as absent, it is probably because their hearts aren't pure enough to discern the signs of his presence and action. Often we are blinded by self-love!

Jesus speaks of purity of *heart*. This is true purity, not the ritual purity to which the Pharisees were attached (avoiding impure foods, faithfully performing rites of external purification). Always, and particularly in the Sermon on the Mount, Jesus draws our attention to the heart—to what is intimate, the deepest intentions and dispositions, and not only the exterior conduct in conformity with rules.

PURITY OF HEART IN THE OLD TESTAMENT

Like other ideas present in the gospel, this one has roots in the Old Testament. The notion of a "pure heart,"

---

3. Jn 17:3.

present throughout the Psalms, the prophets, and other texts, is often linked to several other ideas.

Uprightness—rectitude and sincerity—is one of these. The pure-hearted person is the just man or woman, the *tadiq*, one who sincerely seeks to please God, obey him, and fulfill his commandments. This is opposed to hypocrisy and duplicity. It is characteristic of someone whose external demeanor reflects interior righteousness in all things. This is what Jesus says of Nathaniel: "*Behold, an Israelite indeed, in whom is no guile!*"[4] Those who are pure of heart desire nothing except to please God, have no will other than God's will.

Purity is also related to *simplicity*, as opposed to the idea of mixing, of complication. It implies a love of God and neighbor that isn't tied up in other things, in calculations and human reasoning. It is something like a well-ironed sheet, without creases and folds but smooth, open to God and available to his action instead of folded in on itself.

This being folded in on oneself is opposed to purity of heart. An impure heart is forever looking at itself instead of at God. The craze for "selfies" is a kind

---

4. Jn 1:47.

of symbol of this obsessive preoccupation with one-self and one's image in the eyes of others. As such, it is profoundly opposed to biblical purity. A pure heart is turned toward God, not the self. Indeed, of all man-made idols, the self is worst of all. Nothing is more stifling, more depressing, than narcissistic love of self. And nothing is more liberating than forgetting oneself in order to give one's heart entirely to God.

The third idea closely linked to purity is *unity*. A pure heart is a heart unified by the love of God, entirely oriented toward God, rather than divided by a million contradictory desires or shared between God and idols. In one of the Psalms there is this beautiful expression: "*Teach me thy way, O LORD . . . unite my heart to fear thy name.*"[5]

This unification of the heart by God's love is the central aim of the Shema Israel prayer that pious Jews recite twice a day, quoting Deuteronomy: "*Hear, O Israel: The LORD our God is one LORD; and you shall love the LORD your God with all your heart, and with all your soul, and with all your might.*"[6] God is one. In lov-ing him wholeheartedly men and women realize unity of heart and existence.

---

5. Ps 86:11.
6. Dt 6:4–5.

Purity of heart does not consist in having an absolutely perfect heart, without wounds or faults (no such human heart exists), but a heart *entirely dedicated* to God. Its opposite, according to the prophets, is a shared heart, undecided and irresolute. A person with such a heart has not really made a choice between God and all else, has not put all his or her confidence and love in God.

In the story of the sacrifice on Mount Carmel (in the first book of Kings), Elijah, the only prophet who remains true to God, is opposed by 450 prophets of Baal. He castigates the people in these words: "*How long will you go limping with two different opinions? If the LORD is God, follow him, but if Ba'al, then follow him.*"[7]

Elijah reproaches the people for not deciding on God but instead hesitating between God and the idols. In the morning we offer sacrifice to YHWH, but, not really sure that will work, we burn a little incense to Baal that afternoon. Surely one of them will listen to us! A priest who heard me preach on this subject commented, "Some of my parishioners do exactly that. They come to Mass Sunday morning, and Sunday

---

7. 1 Kgs 18:21.

afternoon they consult the fortune teller. They're hedging their bets."

An impure heart lacks fullness of faith in God. In Acts, Peter speaks of the pagans whose hearts were cleansed by faith.[8] A pure-hearted person has truly chosen to believe fully in God, hope fully in him, and love him with all his or her heart. Teresa of Avila speaks often of *determination*, especially as it is manifested in faithfulness to prayer. Purity of heart does not lie in being perfect but in being determined for God especially through faith and prayer.

We see this in Psalm 51, a beautiful psalm of penitence, in which David asks God to forgive him for his sins: "*Hide thy face from my sins, and blot out all my iniquities. Create in me a clean heart, O God, and put a new and right spirit within me.*"[9]

There are two wonderful ideas here. First, a pure heart is the fruit of a new creation; only God's power and grace can give purity of heart, reorienting human hearts fully toward God. Second, purity of heart is linked to the idea of a renewed and strengthened spirit which has decided to believe, to hope, and to love again: here is the essence of purity of heart.

---

8. Act 15:9.
9. Ps 51:9–10.

The Old Testament sometimes speaks of pure or impure "lips." Isaiah says: *"Woe is me! For I am lost; for I am a man of unclean lips, and I dwell in the midst of a people of unclean lips; for my eyes have seen the King, the LORD of hosts!"*[10] And Zephaniah: *"Yea, at that time I will change the speech of the peoples to a pure speech, that all of them may call on the name of the LORD and serve him with one accord."*[11] Pure lips invoke God, while impure ones praise the idols. Purity is above all a matter of orientation: toward what and whom are my hope, my prayer, my desire directed? Nothing purifies the heart so much as praising and blessing God. A grateful heart is a pure heart.

Your Body is Your Heart

Purity of heart, though first of all concerned with the relationship with God, obviously has fundamental implications for relationships with others: that they be loved, respected, and never used as instruments to serve our desires and interests. I owe the other person uncon-ditional respect for his or her freedom, vocation, heart,

---

10. Is 6:5.

11. Zep 3:9.

emotions, and body, never treating him or her as a mere object and always acknowledging his or her uniqueness. Here especially is the significance of "purity" in the emotional and sexual domains.

But not only there—despite the tendency to reduce purity to what has to do with sex. Other forms of impurity, manifested in lack of respect for others and ourselves, dishonesty, egoism and pride, can be more serious than sexual weakness. (The Lord often uses temptations and falls in regard to sex to rid us of pride, which is a much worse sin. It's a phrase a bishop once said of the Jansenist nuns of Port Royal: "pure like angels and proud like demons.")

Still, let's not be complacent about lack of purity of heart in the sexual domain. The "commodifying" of the body, the hyper-eroticization of relationships, the disappearance of the least hint of modesty and chastity in the media—in short, a total loss of restraint in the sexual domain—is now doing terrible harm to people, to youth, to families. We may not sit by silently and idly in the face of this assault on the human person, which is destroying couples and families. We put much effort into cleaning our rivers and fighting air pollution but do nothing about this far worse, far more virulent pollution now overwhelming Western civilization.

There can be no purity of heart without purity of the body. The two are closely linked. The body is the jewel box of the heart, of interiority, of intimacy; it is the medium through which "heart" is expressed.

Christianity is accused of being a religion that disdains the body. It's true Christian societies have sometimes been influenced by narrow, even negative views of the body and sexuality, but these are flotsam of history and not consistent with essential biblical revelation. Which has more disdain for the body—a religion that believes in bodily resurrection, and bodily participation in God's glory, the body as a member of the body of Christ, a temple of the Spirit, and a place where the gift of eternal life is given, the body as an instrument of sacramental worship and praise through song, gesture, and dance, as well as a means of marvelous communion among people, the favored instrument of service and charity; or is it a society in which the body is exposed naked on billboards and magazines, constantly used as a marketing tool, reduced to a marketable product by pornography, sex trafficking, and surrogacy, covered by atrocious tattoos, invaded by piercings, delivered to surgeon's scalpels in order to conform to the dictates of fashion or the caprice of sex change? The answer is clear.

Christian purity in the physical domain isn't just a negative thing, concerned with avoiding certain conduct. It is above all positive, concerned with discovering the splendor of the body, its human and spiritual beauty, as St. John Paul II did.

The Christian writers of antiquity like St. Augustine expanded on the biblical affirmation that humankind is made in the image of God and on the structure of the soul, in which they discovered an analogy with the Trinity. The three powers of the soul (memory, intelligence, and will) are likened to the three persons of the Trinity, Father, Son, and Holy Spirit.[12] Similarly, I suggest we develop a Trinitarian theology of the body. Like the Father, the body is *memory*, containing the history and identity of the person. Like the Son, it is *language*, an extraordinary and precious way of communicating (sometimes the last and only way to communicate with a dying person is by holding his or her hand). Like the Holy Spirit, it is *presence*—what makes the mystery of the person present in the world. And through the Eucharist God is present among us *bodily* until the end of time.

---

12. Catherine of Siena. *The Dialogue*, trans. Suzanne Noffke, OP (New York: Paulist Press, 1980), loc. 3711–3713.

PURITY OF HEART MEANS HAVING MERCY TOWARD OTHERS

It is no accident that the Beatitude of purity of heart follows the Beatitude of mercy, for purity of heart finds expression in mercy. Mercy purifies hearts as nothing else does. Jesus told the Pharisees: "*Give for alms those things which are within; and behold, everything is clean for you!*"[13] This is echoed in a wonderful saying of Isaac the Syrian, a monk who was bishop of Nineveh in the seventh century: "*When he sees all men in a good light, without any one appearing to him unclean or defiled, such a man has really reached purity.*"[14]

The highest level of purity of heart is not judging anyone any more.

> And what is the sum of purity? A heart full of mercy unto the whole created nature.... And what is a merciful heart? He replied: The burning of the heart unto the whole creation, man, fowls and beasts, demons and whatever exists so that by the recollection and the sight of them the eyes shed tears on account of

13. Lk 11:41.

14. Isaac of Ninevah, *Oeuvres spirituelles* (Brussels: Desclée de Brouwer, 1981), 85th discourse. *https://archive.org/stream/IsaacOfNinevehMystic Treatises/isaac_of_nineveh_mystical_treatises_djvu.txt*

the force of mercy which moves the heart by great compassion. Then the heart becomes weak and it is not able to bear hearing or examining injury or any insignificant suffering of anything in the creation. And therefore even in behalf of the irrational beings and the enemies of truth and even in behalf of those who do harm to it, at all times he offers prayers with tears that they may be guarded and strengthened; even in behalf of the kinds of reptiles, on account of his great compassion which is poured out in his heart without measure, after the example of God.[15]

Keep Your Heart Pure during Trials and Suffering

The struggle for purity of heart requires keeping one's heart free from anything that can harm it by causing it to lose its capacity for love. This is true especially of negative thoughts: judgments, bitterness, sadness, worry, etc. Scripture points to a strong connection between the heart and thought, and speaks often of "*the thoughts of the heart.*" Thought gives direction to the heart and determines action, which is why it is important.

---

15. Ibid., 81st discourse, p 395.

Jesus says, "*There is nothing outside a man which by going into him can defile him; but the things which come out of a man are what defile him.*"[16] It is not the things that come to us from outside us that do us harm, but our interior reaction, starting with our thoughts.

It is unavoidable that we should react negatively to sufferings and deceptions and shocking events of all sorts. But it is imperative that we not give free reign to these thoughts, not dwell on them, but should displace them with positive thoughts of faith, hope, and love. This is an essential aspect of the spiritual struggle. Even the verse in Psalm 137, "*O daughter of Babylon, you devastator! Happy shall he be who requites you with what you have done to us! Happy shall he be who takes your little ones and dashes them against the rock!*"[17] is interpreted by the Fathers of the Church to mean: Happy are those who dash the negative and destructive thoughts that spring from the heart (children of Babylon), against the stone which is the name of Jesus. Whether they be negative or positive, our thoughts have consequences by determining our concrete decisions, and we must take them very seriously.

---

16. Mk 7:15.
17. Ps 137:8–9.

For example, suffering easily becomes accusation, bitterness, judgment, pessimism, discouragement, worry, etc. This, not suffering itself, is what darkens the soul and causes harm. Thus, in difficult times we need to keep our hearts pure by tending to our thoughts. It is certainly not easy, but it is necessary. In particular we should be vigilant in regard to judgmental thoughts about others and anxious thoughts. We cannot hope to avoid them altogether, but embracing and nourishing them leads to disaster.

Here is a consideration that may make this struggle easier. The Beatitude "Happy are the pure of heart because they will see God" could be turned the other way around: "Happy are those who see God, for they will keep their hearts pure." The most powerful safeguard of pure heart is *the spirit of faith* by which we see God's hand in everything that comes to us, including the bad things which are not the result of human fault or error but of the mysterious action of the divine will. This is what the saints did, and made them free. In a letter to her sister Agnes, Thérèse of Lisieux compares herself to a weak reed, but "*[one that] cannot break since, no matter what happens to it, it wants only to see the gentle hand of its Jesus.*"[18]

---

18. Thérèse of Lisieux, *General Correspondence Volume One*, trans. John Clarke, OCD (Washington, D.C.: ICS, 1982), LT 55.

7

HAPPY ARE
THE PEACEMAKERS

According to his promise we wait for new heavens and
a new earth in which righteousness dwells. Therefore,
beloved, since you wait for these, be zealous to be found
by him without spot or blemish, and at peace.[1]

For thus said the Lord GOD, the Holy One of Israel, "In
returning and rest you shall be saved; in quietness and
in trust shall be your strength." And you would not.[2]

Let the peace of Christ rule in your hearts, to which
indeed you were called in the one body.[3]

The Beatitude of the peacemakers is the seventh,
and not by chance. In the biblical tradition the number
seven indicates perfection, fullness. God created the

---

1. 2 Pt 3:13–14.
2. Is 30:15.
3. Col 3:15.

world in six days and rested on the seventh, happy to contemplate the beauty and goodness of his works. "*He saw that it was good!*" The seventh day, the Sabbath, is the day when humankind is invited to rest in a particular way and embrace God's peace: "*Shabbat Shalom*" is the Jewish salutation for the Sabbath, expressing a wish for peace that is not merely the absence of conflict but order, fullness, accomplishment, happiness. The opposite of peace isn't only war but frustration, interior emptiness, dissatisfaction, worry.

Placing this Beatitude seventh signifies that one who lives according to the six that precede it will receive the grace of peace and will be empowered to spread this peace around himself or herself, thereby realizing their baptismal vocation to be children of God. All too often, what we spread, sometimes without knowing it, are our fears, worries, partisan attitudes, and agitation. But by virtue of our Christian vocation, we are called to transmit God's peace. St. Seraphim of Sarov says: "*Acquire interior peace and a multitude will find salvation through you.*"

The Beatitudes point to the true path of purification. Let's briefly consider how each one leads to peace of heart.

Poverty of heart. Without this virtue, one can never be at peace and always in conflict with ourselves or others. Attachment to riches, whether material, moral, or spiritual, will always be a source of worry. The poor in heart are supported entirely by God, have nothing to defend, nothing to lose, nothing to conquer. And so they find peace. Humility leads to peace, while pride is one of the worst enemies of interior peace. "*The meek shall possess the land, and delight themselves in abundant prosperity.*"[4]

Tears and consolation. Someone who has gone through trials and tasted divine consolation receives the grace of peace that can be shared with others.

Meekness. Gospel meekness, the renunciation of violence, bitterness and anger, obviously leads to peace.

Hunger and thirst for justice. Those who seek the justice of the Kingdom will be filled and therefore at peace: "*Great peace have those who love thy law.*"[5]

Mercy. One who is merciful will find peace, while someone who doesn't forgive will never be at peace.

Purity of heart. One who loves with a true and disinterested love will find peace, while someone who seeks his or her own satisfaction will never be satisfied or peaceful.

---

4. Ps 37:11.
5. Ps 119:165.

The Urgency of Peace

We cannot transmit peace unless we have it in our hearts. In the Letter to the Colossians, Paul says: "*Let the peace of Christ rule in your hearts, to which indeed you were called in the one body.*"[6] Embracing his peace is a true calling addressed to us by God. Being at peace is an essential element of the Christian vocation. And there is a spiritual urgency here. As the Church advances through history, it is called to live each of the Beatitudes more and more perfectly, but especially the seventh. Christ strongly invites us to be at peace, embracing God's peace in our hearts.

The first duty of a Christian is not to be perfect or resolve all problems, but to be at peace. As Etty Hillesum wrote in 1942: "*Ultimately, we have just one moral duty: to reclaim large areas of peace in ourselves, more and more peace, and to reflect it toward others. And the more peace there is in us, the more peace there will also be in our troubled world.*"[7]

Someone whose heart is not at peace will be vulnerable to the force of division and all the cycles of fear

---

6. Col 3:15.

7. *Etty Hillesum: An Interrupted Life and Letters from Westerbork* (New York: Holt, 1996), p. 218.

and violence that trouble the world. Whatever within me is not at peace gives a foothold to evil—it is like a gate left open for the demons and those forces of division that they use to draw the world to its damnation. The history of the twentieth century shows this happening again and again—for example, in Europe during the Second World War or in Rwanda during its violent years, when even people who considered themselves good Christians and were active in the Church performed acts of violence or cowardice of which they would not have dreamed themselves capable. For hearts not truly at peace in God, hearts ruled by fear or defense mechanisms and abruptly plunged into situations filled with evil, violence, hate, and division, where social pressures are mounting—such hearts, I say, are unable to resist doing evil themselves. There are times when the existence of a good moral code is by itself not enough.

Peace, a Divine Promise

Acquiring peace, through perhaps requiring much work, is more like placing one's trust in a promise than engaging in an ascetical discipline. Jesus' long Last Supper discourse in the Gospel of John is relevant here. At the start of chapter 14 we find him telling the Apostles: "*Let not your hearts be troubled!*" And a little later we find, "*Peace I leave with you; my peace I give to you; not as the world gives do I give to you. Let not your hearts be troubled, neither let them be afraid.*"[8] The peace Jesus promises isn't worldly peace (tranquility when things are going well, problems have been resolved and desires satisfied—peace of a kind that is in fact rather rare) but can be received and experienced even in humanly difficult situations, because God is its source and foundation. At the end of chapter 16, just before his priestly prayer to the Father, Jesus tells his disciples: "*I have said this to you, that in me you may have peace. In the world you have tribulation; but be of good cheer, I have overcome the world.*"[9] The purpose of all he has said, his spiritual testament, is to establish peace for those who believe.

This peace does not come from outside, from the world. It comes from our communion in faith and love with Jesus, the Prince of Peace. It is a fruit of prayer. As with all the Beatitudes, the matter of the Beatitude of peace is above all a divine quality. God is an ocean of peace, and it is in intimate union with him through

---

8. Jn 14:27.

9. Jn 16:33.

prayer that our hearts find peace. Sometimes it is urgent, indeed a duty, to pray for the return of peace. This experience of prayer as a place of peace is one of the criteria for discerning the authenticity of our prayer life. It doesn't matter that our prayer is poor or dry if it brings the fruits of peace. But if this is not the case, we may need to ask ourselves whether we are praying enough or in the right way.

Paul's letter to the Philippians contains yet another of the many beautiful passages in Scripture promising peace:

> The Lord is at hand. Have no anxiety about anything, but in everything by prayer and supplication with thanksgiving let your requests be made known to God. And the peace of God, which passes all understanding, will keep your hearts and your minds in Christ Jesus.[10]

WHY LOOK FOR PEACE?

The quest for interior peace is far more than a search for psychological tranquility. It is concerned with opening up ourselves to the action of God. One needs to understand a simple but spiritually important truth: the more

---

10. Phil 4:5–7.

one tends toward peace, the more God's grace can act in one's life. As a placid lake mirrors the sun, so a peaceful heart receives the action and motions of the Spirit.

But "*the enemy detests this peace. For he knows that this is the place where the spirit of God dwells, and that God now desires to accomplish great things in us. Consequently he employs his most devilish means to destroy this peace.*"[11] St. Francis de Sales says something similar: "*Because love resides only in peace, be careful always to keep the holy peace of heart that I so often recommend to you.*"[12] Only a peaceful heart can truly love. Thus we must try our best to preserve peace of heart, struggling against worry, anxiety, and spiritual agitation. This peace is an indispensable condition of allowing God to call us to grow in love and fulfillment.

Peace is needed also to discern well. If one is not at peace but is instead troubled, anxious, or agitated, swept by a torrent of emotions, one lacks an objective view of reality and is tempted to take a negative view of everything and call into question its value. When we are at peace, however, we see clearly.

---

11. Dom Lorenzo Scupoli. *The Spiritual Combat*, trans. William Lester and Robert Paul Mohan (London: Catholic Way Publishing, 2013), EPUB.

12. *Letter to the Abbess of Puy d'Orbe.*

Diadochus of Photike puts it like this: "*In every way, therefore, and especially through peace of soul, we must make ourselves a dwelling-place for the Holy Spirit. Then we shall have the lamp of spiritual knowledge burning always within us.*"[13] St. Ignatius of Loyola understood this very well; he distinguished between periods of "consolation" and "desolation" in the spiritual life, and counseled against making serious decisions in the latter state, saying instead that one should stand by decisions reached during the last "peaceful spell."[14]

From this we can deduce the following rule of conduct: When a problem causes you to lose your peace, don't hurry to resolve the problem in hopes of regaining peace, but first regain a modicum of peace and then see what can be done about the problem. In this way one avoids hasty, precipitous decisions ruled by fear and doesn't make the mistake of tormenting oneself trying to solve a problem about which one can do nothing, as people so often do. But how to regain this modicum of peace? Basically, by putting oneself in God's hands in fervent prayer, making acts of faith and

---

13. Patristic reading of the Liturgy of the Hours for Wednesday of the Fourth week of Ordinary Time.

14. *The Spiritual Exercises of St. Ignatius of Loyola.* Fifth Rule.

hope, and meditating on Scripture passages that invite one to trust. And sometimes by opening one's heart to somebody who can help.

THE NEED FOR A SABBATH OF THE SOUL

Peacemakers will be called children of God because they resemble the Father who is God of Peace. They receive the ineffable divine peace and spread it around them.

The Christian life is paradoxical; it often requires an effort, a struggle, and it obliges us to struggle fiercely against sin. Those who give themselves to God never lack work—they have more work than they want. The Gospels show that the few moments when Jesus took his disciples aside for a little rest, they rarely succeeded, for the crowds rushed after them in their place of retreat. And yet the Lord's burden is easy and his load is light, and he doesn't leave his followers without the rest that all people need.[15]

Being a believer calls for working with generosity but also knowing how to rest in God. There is a "Sabbath of the soul," a heart's rest that God prepares for his children, and it is absolutely indispensable that we enter into it,

---

15. Mt 11:28–30.

lest our lives go off the track. There is a real danger of being overwhelmed by activism and stress, of losing one's way, even though the world is actually a gift to be embraced rather than a work to be done. We are at risk of claiming God's place—forgetting that we are useless servants, and so losing our sense of gratitude and wonder and contemplation.

This is a big problem today. Pressure to produce, anxiety about the future, prideful craving for success, the influx of communication technology are creating workaholics who don't know how to enjoy physical, psychological, and spiritual repose. It's alarming to see society losing its appreciation for the weekly day of rest when work is set aside and people cultivate the values of thanksgiving, generosity, prayer, community, and familial relationships as gifts from God. Jewish tradition affirms that it's not we human beings who keep the Sabbath, but the Sabbath that keeps us humans by celebrating the fundamental values of life. Without the Sabbath, we are handed over to the idols of productivity and dehumanized.

True, our lives can never be perfectly balanced nor can we always find the repose and relaxation we may seek. But there is one sort of rest God will never refuse us—restful self-abandonment to his love. Think of

Psalm 116, which Acts shows us Peter citing in support of his testimony to Jesus' resurrection:

> I keep the LORD always before me; because he is at my right hand, I shall not be moved. Therefore my heart is glad, and my soul rejoices; my body also dwells secure. For thou dost not give me up to Sheol, or let thy godly one see the Pit.[16]

Even in stormy times we can be like little children peacefully asleep in the arms of their Father as Jesus in the boat during the storm on the lake.[17]

The Beatitude points to a profound link between peace and repose and being a child of God. It is the Son himself, Jesus, who causes us to enter into the repose of God. He brings the mystery of the Shabbat to its fruition. He is our true peace, for in him we are reconciled with God, with our brothers and sisters, with ourselves, with life. St. Paul in Ephesians says Christ made peace through his cross.[18] He is the Promised Land where God's people find rest. He is the Good Shepherd who leads us to the waters of repose to renew our souls.[19]

16. Ps 16:8–10; cf. Acts 2:22–32.
17. Cf. Lk 8:22–25.
18. Eph 2:14–18.
19. Ps 23:2.

The Letter to the Hebrews, citing Psalm 95, exhorts us not to allow our hearts to be hardened by unbelief and to enter today into the rest prepared for us by God.[20] Happy are those who permit God to rest in their hearts, who do not *"get tired of God"* through disbelief. Happy are those whose hearts repose in the heart of Jesus and who offer him their hearts as a place of rest. Happy are those whose pacified hearts also become a place of rest for all their brothers and sisters, embracing them with tenderness and goodness.

Here is a paradox of love: Love is never at rest, because it is always active, but at the same time it is true rest. He who loves rests in the loved one and offers the love of his heart as a place of rest as St. John so often tells us.

If we allow ourselves to be made peaceful by God, growing in faith, hope, and love and in friendship with Jesus, the Prince of Peace, we shall become peacemakers. By offering our hearts as places of peace and repose to those whom the Lord causes us to encounter, we travel the paths of our lives, welcoming them and loving them tenderly, just as they are, offering them some of the consolation, repose, and peace

---

20. Heb 3:7–11.

whose source is in God. Such peace can be hard to find in today's world, and helping others find it is a magnificent part of our vocation.

Only when the peace of God reigns in our hearts can we live the eighth Beatitude, the acceptance of persecution as a grace.

8

HAPPY ARE THOSE PERSECUTED FOR JUSTICE

If you are reproached for the name of Christ, you are blessed, because the spirit of glory and of God rests upon you.[1]

For one is approved if, mindful of God, he endures pain while suffering unjustly.[2]

But even if you do suffer for righteousness' sake, you will be blessed. Have no fear of them, nor be troubled.[3]

The Disciple and the Master

The last two Beatitudes, the eighth and the ninth, have the same subject: persecution for justice. Eight is the

---

1. 1 Pt 4:14.
2. 1 Pt 2:19.
3. 1 Pt 3:14.

number of the Resurrection, the eschatological advent of the Kingdom. But this is an advent that takes place through patient nurture and the sorrows of labor, of which the number nine is a symbol.

> Blessed are those who are persecuted for righteousness' sake, for theirs is the kingdom of heaven.

> Blessed are you when men revile you and persecute you and utter all kinds of evil against you falsely on my account. Rejoice and be glad, for your reward is great in heaven, for so men persecuted the prophets who were before you.[4]

Lest there be any doubt, the reference to persecution "on my account" makes it clear that this is persecution for Christ. The righteousness or justice envisaged is the justice of which we spoke in reflecting on the fourth Beatitude. This is something far larger than justice in human relationships. It is the truth and faithfulness of God, considered in relation to humanity's salvation.

As the last Beatitude, the conclusion, this one has special significance. As is also true of the first Beatitude, this one promises as its reward the possession of

---

4. Mt 5:10–12.

the Kingdom—God's love fully reigning in our lives. What can we imagine more splendid than this?

Here it is repeated a second time, and addressed more directly than before to the disciples and the others who hear Jesus: "Happy are *you* . . ." Here, pushed to its extreme, is the paradox of the Beatitudes: happiness—indeed, the urging to rejoice and be glad—lies at the heart of that humanly least gratifying of situations, the experience of persecution, insult, and infamous slander.

This is the culmination of the way mapped out by the Beatitudes, the summit of the Holy Spirit's work in our lives: strength to embrace suffering for Christ as a good thing, to welcome the Cross as a gift. Here is the ultimate degree of maturity and spiritual freedom, as well as the most powerful witness human beings can give.

The Church has always known persecution, but today it is more prevalent than ever before. The century extending from the Armenian genocide to the executions carried out by the Islamic State has witnessed more victims among the Christian faithful than the twenty previous centuries, and among all Christian bodies. An ecumenism of blood is among the marks of the Church today.

Persecution can take various forms: the shedding of martyrs' blood, social discrimination and restriction, hateful caricatures of Christian faith in the media, the exclusion of religion from the public square, sneers by teachers and schoolmates aimed at a teenager who affirms that he or she is a Christian, misunderstandings and conflicts within families when some member or members attempt to live the Christian vocation, and much else.

Often, too, especially in Western countries, we see at work very insidious forms of persecution, involving not open persecution but the defaming and denying of Christian values. To be sure, we must avoid having a persecution complex and retreating into a sort of ghetto for protection against the modern world. But that said, it's simply a fact that living in conformity with gospel values and the teaching of the Church isn't easy today. Parents are all too aware of this when they are forced to confront the conflict between the world view and values they try to transmit to their children and those on offer at school and in the media.

Jesus clearly announced:

> Before all this they will lay their hands on you and persecute you, delivering you up to the synagogues and prisons, and you will be brought before kings and governors for my name's sake. This will be a time for you to bear testimony.[5]

---

5. Lk 21:12–13.

And, he said, there should be no surprise about this. "'*A servant is not greater than his master.' If they persecuted me, they will persecute you*"[6] In fact—and alarmingly timely now: "*The hour is coming when whoever kills you will think he is offering service to God.*"[7]

CONTINUITY WITH THE OLD COVENANT

Like the other Beatitudes, the eighth is rooted in the Old Covenant. The reality of persecution is found in different forms: the figure of the just man persecuted because he is faithful to living and announcing the word of God (the prophet Jeremiah is a good example), the people of God who suffer for being different (persecutions to which Israel was subject, as in Exodus, the book of Esther, or the book of the martyrs of Israel). Here we notice a characteristic of persecution: it is hostility that does not have its ultimate source in historic, social, political or other such causes, but in hatred of God and an attempt by the Adversary to destroy God's plan by attacking his children. Quoting a psalm, Jesus says:

> He who hates me hates my Father also. If I had not done among them the works which no one else did,

---

6. Jn 15:20.
7. Jn 16:2.

they would not have sin; but now they have seen and hated both me and my Father. It is to fulfill the word that is written in their law, "They hated me without a cause."[8]

The result is not just a record of human misfortunes but the manifestation of a ferocious struggle between the mystery of Evil and God's providential plans. The demon opposes the election of Israel and the founding of the Church, as he does all other expressions of divine mercy that work to accomplish salvation. Hatred of Israel, like hatred of Christians, has some human explanations, but those fail to account for it. Its deepest roots are in the spiritual realm—in hostility toward God and his creative and redeeming work.[9] This hostility is described early in the Psalms: *"The kings of the earth set themselves, and the rulers take counsel together, against the LORD and his anointed."*[10]

Acts records that during one of the first persecutions a psalm of trust in God was recited, and then *"the place in which they were gathered together was shaken;*

---

8. Jn 15:23–25.

9. In modern times the rejection of God has turned against such fundamental elements of God's creation as the distinction between the two sexes, male and female, and the family. There is an impetus in the direction of a version of humanity severed from the plan of God.

10. Ps 2:2.

and they were all filled with the Holy Spirit and spoke the word of God with boldness."[11] The Holy Spirit came to the aid of those suffering for the Kingdom.

In the Old Testament, the figure of the prophet or just man who is persecuted, becoming an object of hostility and hatred by all because he belongs to God and proclaims God's word, finds its deepest expression in the passages in Isaiah that concern the Servant. This Servant signifies both a people and an individual, and brings an extraordinary message of hope: the suffering of the just will be the source of holiness for all, including those who so frantically oppose him: "*He makes himself an offering for sin . . . he shall bear their iniquities.*"[12] The prophet Zechariah says the death of the just opens up a source of grace and conversion: "*On that day there shall be a fountain opened for the house of David and the inhabitants of Jerusalem to cleanse them from sin and uncleanness.*"[13]

The suffering of the just, culminating in Jesus' cross, is a scandal, but it is a mysterious part of the history of salvation and God's plan. It is both judgment and salvation, a highlighting of human sin and a source of healing from sin.

---

11. Acts 4:31.
12. Is 53:10–11.
13. Zec 13:1.

The Grace of Suffering for Christ

The New Testament tells us that the prospect of persecution, far from being a cause of worry or sadness, should be a source of trust (in the faithfulness and help of God) and even joy (because of the closeness to Christ it fosters and the future reward it helps bring about). St. James says: "*Count it all joy, my brethren, when you meet various trials.*"[14] And the first letter of Peter has this to say:

> Beloved, do not be surprised at the fiery ordeal which comes upon you to prove you, as though something strange were happening to you. But rejoice in so far as you share Christ's sufferings, that you may also rejoice and be glad when his glory is revealed. If you are reproached for the name of Christ, you are blessed, because the spirit of glory and of God rests upon you. But let none of you suffer as a murderer, or a thief, or a wrongdoer, or a mischief-maker; yet if one suffers as a Christian, let him not be ashamed, but under that name let him glorify God.[15]

---

14. Jas 1:2.
15. 1 Pt 4:12–16.

But how is it that persecution, and the acceptance of martyrdom in particular, is a grace?

First, because it is something like a fire that purifies. It requires a decision—a radical and definitive rupture with the world of sin—and it enables one who suffers to enter directly into the holiness of God. As St. Peter says: "*Since therefore Christ suffered in the flesh, arm yourselves with the same thought, for whoever has suffered in the flesh has ceased from sin.*"[16]

In the New Covenant as in the Old, martyrdom is a way of fulfilling the greatest commandment, the Shema Israel that every pious Jew recites twice daily, morning and night: "*You shall love the LORD your God with all your heart, and with all your soul, and with all your might.*"[17] This participation in Christ's suffering

---

16. 1 Pt 4:1.

17. Dt 6:5. The Talmud recounts the martyrdom of Rabbi Akiba, who was put to death by the Romans. At the moment of his torture, the hour came to recite the Shema Israel. He did it joyfully, to the surprise of the Roman governor who condemned him. Rabbi Akiba replied: "Every day I read this verse: 'you will love the Lord with all your heart, all your soul, and all your power.' I was worried and I said to myself, when will these three things come into my hands? I have loved him with all my heart, I have loved him with all my means, but all my soul hasn't yet been put to the test. Now the time has come to test 'all my soul,' and, now, as the time is come for the reading of the Shema, I haven't failed. That's why I read and am filled with joy."

brings to fulfillment the most ardent faith, hope, and charity. To accept martyrdom witnesses to complete faith in God's faithfulness; it forcefully manifests hope in the resurrection of the body and eternal life; and it is the highest expression of love for someone to love God more than his or her own life. Indeed, this is the greatest act of love of God and neighbor that anyone can make: "*Greater love has no man than this, that a man lay down his life for his friends.*"[18] Here is the ultimate expression of love that we see in Jesus: "*Having loved his own who were in the world, he loved them to the end.*"[19]

The incarnation and Passion of Christ show how much God loves us; and the acceptance of martyrdom shows how humankind, through the grace of Christ, are capable of loving God. During the Christmas season there is a striking change in the color of the vestments, from the white of the Nativity to the red of the feast of St. Stephen. Just a day after the joyful feast of the birth of the Lord, celebrating God's becoming one of us out of love for us, we celebrate the feast of the first martyr. God gave himself entirely to us so that we can completely give ourselves to him. He loves us without

---

18. Jn 15:13.
19. Jn 13:1.

measure so that we can love him without measure, even more than our own lives.

Martyrdom is also a supreme act of love of neighbor. The Christian martyr forgives, prays for those who make him or her suffer, and offers his or her life for their salvation. The martyr carries love of enemies as far as it can go, as the gospel urges be done.

But make no mistake, martyrdom is not an expression of personal heroism or greatness. It is a witness to the power of God active within human weakness, as the preface for the Mass of the martyrs says:

> For the blood of your blessed blessed martyr . . . , poured out like Christ's to glorify your name, shows forth your marvelous works, by which in our weakness you perfect your power and on the feeble bestow strength to bear you witness, through Christ our Lord.

On several occasions in accounts of martyrdoms in the early centuries we find the figure of an acetic who voluntarily comes forward to be judged at a time of persecution, and then, under torture, denies Christ, in contrast with someone else, frequently a frail young woman like St. Blandine of Lyon, whom no one expected to stand up under five minutes of torture, who emerges as the bravest of all.

What explains the beauty and grace of the martyr, the goodness hidden, is the depth of communion with God, that leads St. Ignatius of Antioch on his way to martyrdom to say (in his letter to the Romans), "*Let me be the food of the animals, through which it will be possible for me to find God*"? To suffer martyrdom makes it certain that one will enter the house of the Father forever: "*There is within me a water that lives and speaks, saying to me inwardly: come to the Father.*"

Here is the most profound communion and identification with Christ possible, accomplished, as we say at each Eucharist, "through Him, in Him, and with Him." Each martyrdom reproduces the Passion of Christ. St. Felicity, arrested in Carthage in 202, gave birth to a child in prison just before her martyrdom. To a jailer who said to her, "if you're groaning now, what will you do when you're exposed to the beasts?" she replied: "I'm the one who suffers now, but then, there will be another in me who will suffer for me, because it is for him that I will be suffering."

Martyrdom is the occasion of our most powerful experience of the Spirit's help. As St. Peter says in a passage quoted earlier: "*If you are reproached for the name of Christ, you are blessed, because the spirit of glory and of God rests upon you.*"[20]

---

20. 1 Pt 4:14.

The stories of the martyrs in the first centuries strongly highlight the charismatic aspect of martyrdom. The Holy Spirit is present in those who suffer for Jesus, giving them strength and manifesting itself in the words of wisdom, the prophecies, and the visions that often accompany the moment of martyrdom. The Acts of the Apostles says of St. Stephen: "*He, full of the Holy Spirit, gazed into heaven and saw the glory of God, and Jesus standing at the right hand of God; and he said, 'Behold, I see the heavens opened, and the Son of man standing at the right hand of God.'*"[21] *

Recently I read an account of the assassination of Father Jacques Hammel by an elderly couple who saw it happen. The old priest's throat was slit by two young jihadists while he celebrated the Eucharist at St. Stephen of Rouvray. The jihadists asked the husband to film the act with a cellphone. Then they struck him and he fell to the ground, pretending to be dead. He says: "*I was convinced that I was going to die, but I prayed. I contemplated my life, and I was at peace. I have never been so serene. Completely in peace. I had no remorse, only love in me. In fact, it was a moment of great happiness.*"[22]

---

21. Acts 7:55–56.

22. Interview with the survivors of the attack at the Church of St. Étienne-du-Rouvray in *Famille Chretienne,* September 28, 2016.

To feel such a peace and happiness at such a moment can only be the work of the Holy Spirit. This is testimony to the truth of Jesus' promises.

How to Practice This Beatitude?

Most of us do not live amid the persecution that is a regular occurrence today for some Christian communities in the Middle East. What does practicing this Beatitude mean for us?

First of all, we must be ready. Jesus tells us: "*Watch therefore, for you know neither the day nor the hour.*"[23] He also tells us: "*Watch and pray that you may not enter into temptation; the spirit indeed is willing, but the flesh is weak.*"[24]

Given modern means of persecution, there is no truly safe place. One might be called on to die for the faith at any time and in any place. This does not mean living in constant fear; Jesus insists on that. Nor should we prepare our apologia; the Holy Spirit will be given to us when the time comes. What we need to do is faithfully live our Christian vocation, persevere in prayer, and remain in union with Christ above all.

---

23. Mt 25:13.
24. Mt 26:41.

A few other points about the Christian struggle deserve mention.

One is to pray for Christians who suffer. We benefit from their sacrifice, and we have a duty to help them especially by praying. If one member of the body suffers, all members share the suffering, as St. Paul says. And yet we readily forget them, as happened during the Communist persecutions in the Eastern Europe, when the suffering of Christian there sometimes received little attention from the Christian communities in the West.

We also need to accept the fact that Christian life is a combat, a struggle to be faithful, to resist temptation, to undergo continuing conversion, to serve God and proclaim the gospel in a variety of ways. "*Take your share of suffering as a good soldier of Christ Jesus,*" Paul tells Timothy.[25] Everyone who does it is aware that many difficulties plague any attempt to announce the word of God: material problems, interior anguish and fatigue, temptations of all sorts. Without seeing spiritual warfare everywhere (if something doesn't work, we may just need to change the batteries), it's a fact that something besides human causes are at work in the vicissitudes of life in service of Christ.

---

25. 2 Tm 2:3.

People who don't believe in the devil are, I suspect, people who haven't really lived or preached the gospel seriously. St. Paul speaks about spiritual combat in a famous passage in terms fully applicable to present realities:

> Be strong in the Lord and in the strength of his might. Put on the whole armor of God, that you may be able to stand against the wiles of the devil. For we are not contending against flesh and blood, but against the principalities, against the powers, against the world rulers of this present darkness, against the spiritual hosts of wickedness in the heavenly places. Therefore take the whole armor of God, that you may be able to withstand in the evil day, and having done all, to stand.[26]

One ought not be frightened or see the devil's hand in everything (that would be giving him too much credit). But one should be realistic about the war the Church is fighting and trust God's promises with absolute confidence. As St. Paul told Titus, the heart of the combat is "*the good fight of the faith*."[27] We need to have Thérèse

---

26. Eph 6:10–13.
27. 1 Tm 6:12.

of Lisieux's attitude, as in her prayer to Jesus: "*I want to love you like a little child, I want to fight like a brave warrior.*"[28]

Let me emphasize one aspect of this struggle: sometimes you're going to be treated unfairly. Yes, we need to resist all forms of injustice, and we are entitled to claim and to defend our rights, but don't expect to be treated always and only as you deserve. St. Peter told Christian slaves that having to bear patiently with injustice, in love and imitation of Christ, was sometimes part of their vocation.

> For one is approved if, mindful of God, he endures pain while suffering unjustly. For what credit is it, if when you do wrong and are beaten for it you take it patiently? But if when you do right and suffer for it you take it patiently, you have God's approval. For to this you have been called, because Christ also suffered for you, leaving you an example, that you should follow in his steps. He committed no sin; no guile was found on his lips. When he was reviled, he did not revile in return; when he suffered, he did not threaten; but he trusted to him who judges justly.

---

28. Thérèse of Lisieux, *The Poetry of St. Thérèse of Lisieux,* trans. Donald Kinney, OCD (Washington, D.C.: ICS, 1995), PN 36.

He himself bore our sins in his body on the tree, that we might die to sin and live to righteousness. By his wounds you have been healed. For you were straying like sheep, but have now returned to the Shepherd and Guardian of your souls.[29]

An act of discernment is required here: sometimes we should defend ourselves—indeed, it can be necessary and obligatory to do so—but sometimes we must submit to injustice out of love for Jesus. In demanding that we always be treated with perfect justice, we often end by being unjust toward others. It is better to submit to evil than commit it.

Finally, in concluding this treatment of the eighth Beatitude and the spiritual combat, as well as concluding this book, I suggest that we entrust ourselves to Mary. She is our most powerful and effective help in the spiritual combat. Her heart is a haven of peace and hope for all who take refuge in her. Her intercession is powerful before God. Her presence and support are of immense assistance to us in the struggles and temptations we face. Her maternal tenderness is a sweet consolation in our trials. Her faith, her humility, and the

---

29. 1 Pt 2:19–25.

purity of her love, make her unassailable (in the spiritual combat; she is, as the Song of Songs says, "*terrible as an army with banners.*")[30] If we place ourselves under Mary's care, don the armor she proposes—a mantle of white for faith, green for hope, and red for love of which St. John of the Cross speaks,[31] and if we allow ourselves to be enlisted in the army of the poor and the little ones whom she summons and assembles under her banner today for the combat of the last days, nothing can defeat us, and we shall always have the grace to rise again and resume the struggle until the ultimate victory of Love.

Mary lived each of the Beatitudes perfectly, and she helps us understand and practice them effectively. The treasure of the mother belongs to the child, as Thérèse of Lisieux says,[32] and if we give ourselves entirely to her, she will give herself entirely to us and share with us the riches that she has received from God. Through her we shall become poor in heart, humble and meek; in her arms we shall be consoled, she will make us hungry and thirsty for God, will make us good and merciful, will

---

30. Song 6:4.

31. "The Dark Night, Book 2.21" in *The Collected Works.*

32. Thérèse of Lisieux, *Poetry*, PN 54.

share with us the purity of her heart, will establish us in a profound peace to be shared with those around us. She will give us the grace of being strong in the combat and embracing the Cross as a grace. She will open wide the gates of the Kingdom and of true happiness.

WORKS CITED

Cantalamessa, Raniero. *Life in Christ: A Spiritual Commentary on the Letter to the Romans*. Translated by Frances Lonergan Villa. Collegeville, Minn.: Liturgical Press, 2016. EPUB.

Catherine of Siena. *The Dialogue*.

de Bar, Catherine Mectilde. *Adorer et Adhérer*. Paris: Éditions du Cerf, 1994.

de Sales, Francis. *Introduction to the Devout Life*. San Francisco: Ignatius Press, 2015. EPUB.

Dostoyevsky, Fyodor. *The Brothers Karamazov*. Translated by Constance Garnett. Mineola, N.Y.: Dover, 2005.

el-Maskîne, Matta. L'expérience de Dieu dans la vie de prière. Bégrolles-en-Mauges, France: Abbaye de Bellefontaine, 1996.

Eudes, John. *The Life and Kingdom of Jesus in Christian Souls*. CreateSpace Independent Publishing, 2013.

Francis, Encyclical *Lumen Fidei* (June 29, 2013), 34.

Hillesum, Etty. *Etty Hillesum: An Interrupted Life and Letters from Westerbork*. New York: Holt, 1996.

Isaac of Ninevah. *Oeuvres spirituelles*. Brussels: Desclée de Brouwer, 1981. *https://archive.org/stream/IsaacOfNinevehMysticTreatises/isaac_of_ nineveh_mystical_treatises_djvu.txt.*

John of the Cross. *The Collected Works of St. John of the Cross*. Translated by Kieran Kavanaugh, OCD, and Otilio Rodriguez, OCD. Washington, D.C.: ICS, 1991. Kindle.

Kowalska, Maria Faustina. *Diary of Saint Maria Faustina Kowalska: Divine Mercy in My Soul*. Stockbridge, Mass.: Marian Press, 2014. Kindle.

Sagne, Jean-Claude. *La quête de Dieu, chemin de guérison*. Paris: Éditions de l'Emmanuel, 2005.

Scupoli, Dom Lorenzo. *The Spiritual Combat*. Translated by William Lester and Robert Paul Mohan. London: Catholic Way Publishing, 2013. EPUB.

Teresa of Avila. *The Book of Her Life*. Translated by Kieran Kavanaugh and Otilio Rodriguez, OCD. Indianapolis: Hackett, 2008.

"The Return of a Soul to a Torturer." *L'Osservatore Romano*, December 12, 2012. *http://www.osservatoreromano.va/en/news/the-return-of-a-soul-to-a-torturer.*

Thérèse of Lisieux. *General Correspondence Volume Two*. Translated by John Clarke, OCD. Washington, D.C.: ICS Publications, 1988.

———. *St. Thérèse of Lisieux: Her Last Conversations*. Translated by John Clarke, OCD. Washington, D.C.: ICS Publications, 1977.

———. *Story of a Soul: The Autobiography of St. Thérèse of Lisieux*. Translated by John Clarke, OCD. Washington, D.C.: ICS Publications, 1996. Kindle.

———. *The Poetry of St. Thérèse of Lisieux*. Translated by Donald Kinney, OCD. Washington, D.C.: ICS, 1995.

Thérèse of Lisieux and Sister Geneviève. *Conseils et souvenirs*. Paris: Les Éditions du Cerf, 2005, p. 81.